6000 Miles Through Wonderland

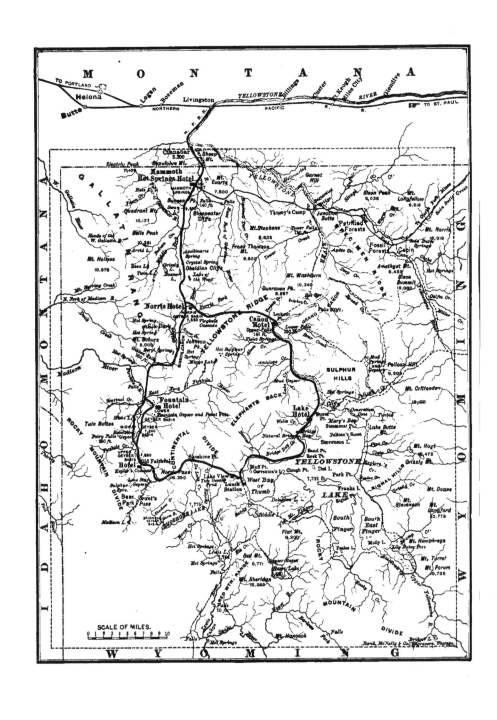

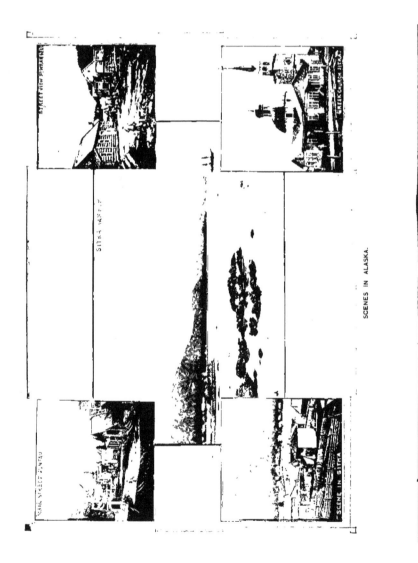

SCENES IN ALASKA.

6,000 Miles Through Wonderland

BEING A DESCRIPTION OF THE MARVELOUS
REGION TRAVERSED BY THE NORTHERN
PACIFIC RAILROAD

_____ By OLIN D. WHEELER

Illustrated from Photos by Haynes

ILLUSTRATIONS.

6,000 Miles Through Wonderland.

SEWARD'S PROPHECY.

> Breathes there a man with soul so dead
> Who never to himself hath said,
> This is my own, my native land?
> —*Scott.*

THE American people are reputed a nation of travelers. The allegation is undoubtedly a true one, and is applicable to no one class alone. Rich and poor, high official and private citizen, the aristocrat and the tramp, each and all exercise the "inalienable right" of an American citizen — and travel. To such an extent is this so that it has been stated, and currently accepted as true, that were it not for the American dollars left in Europe by travelers serious distress would result at many of the points embraced in the continental tour.

In so far as scenery alone is concerned the evidence is beyond dispute that this country can match anything that the old country has to show, and in many cases so far excel it that comparison is out of the question. It is time lost and money thrown away to go from here there to see fine scenery alone. We have more of it than have they.

William H. Seward, prophet, seer, and statesman, pierced the veil far into the future when, standing in 1860 on the platform at the door of the capitol of the State of Minnesota, in St. Paul, he gave utterance in substance to this, at that time, remarkable statement:

I find myself for the first time upon the high land in the center of the continent of North America, equidistant from the waters of Hudson Bay and the Gulf of Mexico. Here is the place, the central place, where the agricultural products of this region of North America must pour out their tributes to the world. I have cast about for the future and ultimate seat of power of North America. I looked to Quebec, to New Orleans, to Washington, San Francisco, and St. Louis for the future seat of power. But I have corrected that view. I now believe that the ultimate last seat of government on this great continent will be found somewhere not far from the spot on which I stand, at the head of navigation of the Mississippi River.

No one starting from this land of the mystic Hiawatha and whirling westward

> To the doorway of the west wind,
> To the portals of the sunset,

through the enchanting Lake Park region of Minnesota, the waving grain fields and delicately sculptured Bad Lands of North Dakota, the vast cattle ranges and mineral-bearing mountains of Montana and Idaho, and the timbered hills and laughing valleys—the joy of the horticulturist—of Washington and Oregon, can for one moment doubt that here indeed is the nucleus of a coming empire.

From the billowy fields of Minnesota and the Dakotas will go forth the bread to feed the nations. From the plateaus and grazing-grounds of North Dakota and Montana will come the beef and mutton and beasts of burden for our own extended domain. From the womb of the mountains of Montana and Idaho will be extracted the precious metals for use in commerce and the arts. From the mountain-bound valleys and plains of Washington and the Puget Sound country will be sent far and wide fruits as luscious as were those which the spies carried back to Joshua from the Land of Canaan.

Here, in this magnificent domain of lofty mountain, sweeping plain, circling valley, pointed cliff, cañoned river, geysered basin, rolling prairie; here, where mountain peaks touch the clouds, rivers throw themselves from dizzy heights into cañon depths below, valleys smile under the benign touch of the Creator, chimneys smoke to the zenith, turning the crudities of the mountains into the polished productions of art, the cattle graze on the thousand hills, the lakes of emerald shimmer and flash in the sunlight, the green fields bend to the evening breeze over leagues of undulating prairie; here is the beginning of an empire destined to exert a vast influence on future civilization.

Well may the patriotic American sing in this year 1893, after a trip through this Indian storyland and white man's wonderland:

> My Country, 'tis of thee,
> Sweet Land of Liberty,
> Of thee I sing.
>
> .   .   .   .
>
> I love thy rocks and rills,
> Thy woods and templed hills,
> My heart with rapture thrills
> Like that above.
>
> .   .   .   .
>
> Long may our land be bright
> With freedom's holy light.
> Protect us with thy might,
> Great God, our King!

SEEN FROM CAR WINDOWS.

ST. PAUL AND MINNEAPOLIS—DULUTH AND THE SUPERIORS—ASHLAND
—MINNESOTA PRAIRIES—LAKE PARK REGION, ETC.

CONSIDERABLE proportion of travelers on American railways have not the time to stop over at the more noted places, nor to make side trips nor excursions to the more interesting points situated a greater or less distance from the immediate line of the railway. What they see must be seen from the windows of the car which for the time being is their home. What they learn of the country through which they ride, its mountains and rivers, plains, valleys, deserts, hamlets, and cities, must be learned from what they see from car windows as they roll onward at thirty and forty miles an hour. This being the case the traveler naturally inquires what he can see in this to some extent limited way as he travels by this or that particular route. Over which line of railway among so many can he, all things considered, see the most, and consequently learn the most, for the expenditure of money he must needs make.

I think I hazard no rash statement when I say that from the time that one takes seat in the cars either at St. Paul or Duluth, the eastern termini of the Northern Pacific, or even at Chicago, the eastern terminus of the Wisconsin Central, its leased line, there is not, with the single exception of a few short hours in the Columbia River Valley, a time that the outlook is not either attractive or interesting.

With the exception noted, the prospect at all times, from a scenic point, varies from the quiet and pleasant pastoral features of the Minnesota and Dakota prairies through the entire category to the grand and uplifting panorama afforded by the passage of the Rocky and Cascade mountains.

ST. PAUL AND MINNEAPOLIS.

Perched upon the rocky bluffs of the Father of Waters, which for long years was its only means of communication with the outer world, St. Paul occupies one of the most sightly spots that nature ever vouchsafed to a city. Below the bluffs and hills which rise in terraces bordering the river in semicircular form lies the lower portion of the city, which is devoted largely to the heavy commercial trade that the city now enjoys. Here also are the railroad yards and freight sheds. The wholesale quarter of the city with its street after street of five and six story buildings, followed by the center devoted to banking and offices, where the commercial temples rise to ten and twelve stories above ground, is most imposing and metropolitan in appearance.

Both north and south of the business center, on the plateaus known as Dayton's Bluff and St. Anthony Hill, are the finer private residences. Summit Avenue, winding over the latter plateau, is now become one of the noted streets of American cities.

St. Paul has projected a fine system of parks. Como Park comprises nearly four hundred acres, and is destined to become one of the handsomest parks of the country.

Near the city, at the confluence of the Mississippi and Minnesota rivers, is Fort Snelling. It is a historic spot, and a beautiful one. The fort is connected with St. Paul both by railroad and electric-car line.

Eight miles up the river, at the noted Falls of St. Anthony, is Minneapolis, a large manufacturing city, and a refined one, spreading abroad the fame of Minnesota and its own reputation through the immense quantities of patent-process flour from its wonderful flour-mills. These mills of Minneapolis are visited by many of the genus tourist, and well repay a visit.

The streets of Minneapolis are wide, her buildings many of them unsurpassed. Besides her great influence as a grain center she is also a great lumber market.

Having for years paid much attention to elaborating a park system, Minneapolis is possessed of a number of parks that will put to blush those of older and larger cities. Lakes Harriet and Calhoun, reached by electric line, are great pleasure resorts.

Contiguous to the city are the noted Minnehaha Falls. These are easily reached by electric line and railroad, and every one who has read Hiawatha should pay this most picturesque spot a visit. Near by the falls is the State Soldiers' Home, bordering the Mississippi River and Minnehaha Creek.

The growth of these twin cities has been phenomenal. In 1880 of less than 100,000 population, in 1890 they held over 300,000 souls.

Minnesota, the "land of the Dacotas," is named from the Minnesota River. The word is difficult of literal translation, but we have the authority of the Historical Society of Minnesota for calling it *sky-tinted water*. The whole State is dotted with lakes. Lakes deep and lakes shallow; lakes large and lakes small; lakes with wooded shores and lakes encircled by waving grasses; lakes with romantic islands and lakes with unbroken and placid surface; but all of them, however varied they may be in configuration and scenic beauty, are of purest crystal water. Nicollet called the country Undine.

RAILWAY ENTRANCE

THE ABERDEEN

FROM WEST SIDE

ST. PAUL

FORT SNELLING AND MINNEAPOLIS.

In one portion of the State these lakes are so numerous that the region is known as the Lake Park region. Through this delightful section the Northern Pacific Railroad winds, and the outlook is at times beautiful.

Leaving St. Paul and Minneapolis the railroad crosses the Mississippi River on a substantial iron bridge, and follows the eastern bank of the Father of Waters to Little Falls. Throughout this distance thrifty villages are passed, situated in the midst of a fine agricultural and manufacturing region.

At Little Falls the railroad again crosses the Mississippi to the western bank, and runs diagonally through a finely timbered country to Staples, where the line from the "Zenith City of the Unsalted Seas," the renowned and now indeed marvelous Duluth, makes junction with the main line.

From Staples the railroad runs westward through the Lake Park region to the famous Red River Valley, the hard-wheat field of the world.

It is estimated that there are from 7,000 to 10,000 lakes in the State of Minnesota, with popular opinion inclining to the latter figure as being nearer correct — which is probably an overestimate.

DULUTH AND THE SUPERIORS.

When Proctor Knott made his speech in the House of Representatives which brought fame to both the little town of Duluth and himself, neither he nor any one else had much expectation that Duluth would ever acquire more than a provincial renown. To-day the "Zenith City of the Unsalted Seas" is indeed a city. Enthroned at the head of our greatest lake, she hurls defiance not only at the twin cities of her own State, but boldly throws down the gauntlet to Chicago, who had long held herself the Mistress of the Lakes.

Duluth is indeed a wonder. With tremendous strides she has moved ahead within the last ten years. The high bluffs that frown down on Superior's bosom have been channeled and planed to make way for streets and fine drives, and the hillside is dotted with the homes and mansions of a people cultured and prosperous. Far up on this hillside also are a church and a high-school building just completed, from whose lofty towers one may gaze far across the waters of the great lake. It is doubtful if outside of New York or Boston, perhaps not there, such a school building can be found in this country, and nearly the same can be said for the church.

Across the water from Duluth, to the east, lie the Superiors. Of this family there are three, Superior, West Superior, and South Superior. West Superior is the largest, and is situated on St. Louis Bay, and has a population of between 15,000 and 20,000. The three places are near together, and connected by railroads. The ground here is as level as it is hilly at Duluth.

This is where the celebrated McDougall Whaleback Steamers are built, and the plant and ship-yard is a very large one.

ASHLAND.

Still eastward on Lake Superior, in Wisconsin, is another city reached by the Northern Pacific. At the head of Chequamegon Bay, overlooking the Apostle Islands, lies Ashland, a city of about 13,000 inhabitants.

It is the great ore-shipping point for the Gogebic Iron Range and is the second largest ore-shipping point in America. It is also a noted health and summer resort. The Hotel Chequamegon, a large, well-appointed hostelry, overlooks the lovely bay, and in summer is well patronized.

This is a region of pine forests, very healthful, and a resort for sufferers from hay fever. There is also hereabouts much fine trout fishing.

RED RIVER VALLEY.

Who has not heard nowadays of the Red River Valley? Its fame is world-wide.

The shepherd in the Highlands of Scotland, the peasant in the sunny fields of France, the dweller on the banks of the Nile, are as deeply interested, practically, in the weather and crop reports from this great wheat land as are we of our own United States.

A strange country this. Three hundred miles long by perhaps sixty wide, it seems to possess few of the attributes of a valley as generally understood.

Among the larger towns and cities of the prairies and the great wheat belt are Little Falls and Brainerd on the Mississippi; Grand Forks and Winnipeg on the Manitoba branch; Moorhead, Fargo, and Jamestown on the main line. Little Falls has a fine water-power, and is largely interested in manufacturing. The Antlers is a good hotel located here, and makes this a pleasant point at which to stop. At Brainerd the Northern Pacific has large shops and a Sanitarium. Moorhead and Fargo are on opposite sides of the Red River, the one in Minnesota, the other in North Dakota. Jamestown is in the valley of the James River, and is the seat of the North Dakota Insane Hospital.

Winnipeg, Manitoba, is a city of 30,000 people, and the most important point in the Canadian Northwest. "The Manitoba," a new hotel, is one of the finest in the Northwest. Winnipeg is the seat of government for the Province of Manitoba.

NORTH DAKOTA BAD LANDS.

The eastern portion of North Dakota is in its general characteristics the counterpart of Western Minnesota. Of an average elevation of from 1,000 to 1,500 feet, as you progress westward to the Missouri River it is an undulating, elevated plain, not plentiful of timber, but of a pleasing appearance, and a good grazing and crop-growing section. As the train steadily rolls westward out of the Red River Valley, the whole land, as far as eye can see, shows that it is eminently the domain of the shepherd and the husbandman.

From an inspection of it there comes to you a feeling, a consciousness, of reserve power. A feeling that as fast as the world's demands increase, here are the means, the broad acres, to supply it.

Leaving the Missouri by the valley of the Heart River, a small stream that twists and doubles upon itself like an acrobat, affording fine glimpses of valley scenery, the road winds westward among rounded, grassy hills, treeless but inviting. We then enter a region possessing physical traits the most remarkable. Scattered throughout the West, both in southern and northern latitudes, are found stretches of country which, from their peculiar configuration and structure, are known to geologists and explorers as the "Mauvaises Terres" or "Bad Lands." A well-known authority says of them: "These are dreary wastes, naked hills with rounded or conical forms, composed of sand, sandy clays, or fine fragments of shaly rocks, with steep slopes; and, yielding to the pressure of the foot, they are climbed only by the greatest toil. . . ." The usual aspect of these Bad Lands is indeed that of a "dreary waste." The writer has ridden through them on horseback, where it seemed as if it were very desolation itself, where the dull, clayey slopes and eroded buttes might well have been thought the huge ash-piles of ancient cities perished from the earth.

West of Dickinson, the Northern Pacific Railroad traverses a portion of these *Mauvaises Terres*, which not only constitutes possibly the most spectacular piece of landscape along the whole length of road, as seen from the car windows, but may with equal truth be pronounced the most glowing and dramatic representation of its kind yet discovered. It is a perfect symphony in form and color.

Such delicacy of tint and perfection of form, coupled at times with the most astounding sculptural effects, and figures the most grotesque, can not, I venture to affirm, be duplicated elsewhere.

In all respects the name Bad Lands is an unfortunate misnomer, and greatly to be regretted so far as this particular region goes. The Sculptured Lands would have been far more to the purpose, for sculpturing it is, on a grand scale. Old Nature simply "turned herself loose," when with fire and hail, frost and snow, and wind and rain, she determined to leave to remotest ages an ideal piece of work for an object lesson in sculpture and architecture.

My first ride through this land of animated lifelessness was taken perched in the cab of a locomotive. As we reached the down grade, and gradually descended into the plutonian realms, the panorama spread forth upon all sides simply beggared description. Doré *might* have been able to paint it, but I fancy he would have been glad when he was through with it.

The horizon fairly teemed with the buttes, cliffs, and bluffs of this weird land. Thicker and more complex they became, and from them, springing aloft in endless array and multiform shapes, were pinnacles, spires, domes, and turrets. In the far distance, wrapped about in a mysterious veil of haze — that soft, beautiful, unreal yet strangely real thing of Western landscape,

Like the indistinct golden and vaporous fleece
Which surrounded and hid the celestials in Greece —

these cliffs became strange creatures of the imagination. Anything that fancy painted them, that they were. Old mediæval ruins, cities gone to decay, castles and watch-towers tumbled into picturesque confusion, walled towns along the border, remnants of conflagration most disastrous — each and all they could be in turn, and in each natural. The region is one where fire and water has each played its part. It seems well settled that the climate was at one time a tropical one, where vegetation flourished to a remarkable degree.

Once the train is well within the Bad Lands, the view becomes circumscribed. Now the detail of form is greater. The road winds about, dodging knolls, edging away from ravines, occasionally going straight through a hill when it can not do otherwise; all the time seeking a way out of this labyrinthian scene, and affording many-sided views of the wonderful forms.

The minarets already . . .
There, certes, in the valley I descry,
Gleaming vermilion, as if they from fire
Had issued.   .   .   .   Eternal fire,
That inward burns, shows them with ruddy flame
Illumed.

Cone-shaped hills, perfect in shape, connected by geometric bluffs, bring to mind military fortifications. We roll past a rounded hill, crowned with a perfect nipple of pink scoria. Then comes a procession of stone men, always in marching order but never moving. Fluted slopes, finely chased mounds, fretted cliffs, hills exquisite in their symmetry, and banded or dashed with vivid Indian red and paler terra cotta, whirl rapidly past. Occasionally a long, narrow ribbon of black lignite can be traced on the hillside, perhaps still smoking from the smoldering fire within. A strange intermingling of the grotesque and symmetric — war-like bastion and fort, ruined towers, nippled peaks, flowing ridges, mottled hills — this.

A tour of this region on horseback, under a guide, if desired, familiar with the locality, would be rich in new and varied experiences to an Easterner.

A week's camping-tour in summer under these balmy skies and in this exhilarating atmosphere would prove a surprising tonic to some exhausted, depleted wreck of manhood. In addition to health and strength regained, a fund of adventure of a mild sort would be obtained from which to regale friends around the hearthstone in the winter. The scenes of the nightly camp fire of the North Dakota prairies might be shifted to the grate fires of Eastern homes.

YELLOWSTONE VALLEY—THE ROCKY MOUNTAINS—HELENA AND
THE BROADWATER.

The valley of the Yellowstone River affords a change in landscape architecture, which, as the valley is ascended, grows more marked with every mile.

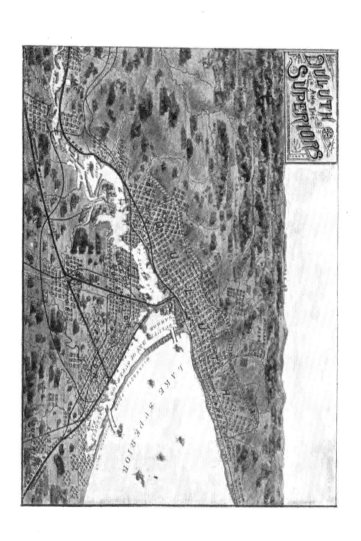

Battle Lake.   Detroit Lake.

MINNESOTA LAKES.

For 340 miles, from Glendive to Livingston, the railroad follows this interesting stream.

The railroad crosses the river three times, but in the greater part of its course follows the south bank. The valley is from five to ten miles in width, flanked by the bluffs characteristic of Western streams. The bluffs themselves are not particularly interesting except in occasional instances, but, in combination with the wide expanse of valley and river, do their part to create a varied outlook. Through this wide, hill-bounded valley the green Yellowstone rolls along, careering as it pleases from one side to the other. Here it leaves a wide sand-bar glistening in the sunlight; there it remorselessly eats away at its banks, which are doomed, sooner or later, to give up the struggle and succumb to the persistent foe. Now it goes pouring its snow-fed waters resistlessly through the bottoms, between a stately avenue of cottonwoods, while the fresh green meadows stretch well back against the more dingy bluffs. The river itself is by all odds the feature of it all, and is one of the very finest of Western rivers. Its rapid current gives it life and energy, while its deep, pure color invests it with an unusual charm for this region.

Miles City and Billings, the former the county seat of Custer County, Mont., and the latter the division terminus of the Yellowstone and Montana divisions, are two important shipping centers for Montana cattle. Both are thriving towns, and a day or two spent here at the proper season will give the tourist a chance to see interesting features of the cattle business.

The upper valley will, however, draw admiration from an anchorite. It becomes more contracted, assumes a wilder and more rugged nature, the river flows over an uneven bottom which imparts its character to the emerald flood itself, while the hills have grown to manhood and are now mountains, standing forth in all their stateliness and strength. Each cutting peak or massive frontlet, as it bears itself proudly aloft, seems to say disdainfully,

> I am monarch of all I survey,
> My right there is none to dispute.

In the very early morning, long before Livingston is reached, we get enlivening views of distant mountains, and refreshing whiffs of invigorating mountain air.

Far away to the north the jagged crests of the Crazy Mountains break upon the vision. Distant at first, and in appearance, as it were, like floating turrets in an azure sea, they gradually reveal themselves, a fine and imposing group of sharply pointed mountains, 10,000 feet high, with long, bare, or thinly wooded flanks, and in places crowned with massive palisades. As the train winds in different directions, this superb old assemblage of crags is an interesting study in the various changes of form which they undergo.

Livingston, a pushing, thriving little city, is situated in the midst of an attractive scene. The valley, here a wide expanse, gradually rises to the base of the mountains which encircle it. The long ridges and cones of the latter, beneath whose feet sleeping snowbanks lie, look down proudly upon the basin below with its bustling town, where not long since solitude reigned supreme. As the train moves onward, following the line of the Park branch road, one sees, in well-framed perspective, through the "Gate of the Mountains" — as some term the cañon from which issues the Yellowstone River — the western slopes of the Absarokas.

Gradually ascending through a mildly mountain country, where rolling hills, smoothed down by water, afford some delicious bits of scenery, Bozeman tunnel, over 3,600 feet long, is reached. Here we are much higher above the sea than one would naturally think. The highest point of the floor of this tunnel is 5,565 feet above old ocean, which is seventeen feet higher than we will be when we arrive at the more celebrated Mullan tunnel beyond Helena.

Leaving Bozeman, a thriving little city of several thousand inhabitants, the wide plain of the Gallatin Valley, noted for its richness and fertility, opens before us. The mountains disperse themselves and loom up afar off through the hazy atmosphere. A wonderful valley is the Gallatin, and like so many other localities on this road, a historic one. Within its sacred precincts the great Missouri River takes its rise. Flowing from the frowning cliffs and forested gulches of the mountains to the south, fed by perennial springs, which in turn come from the never-failing snow-drifts and glaciers above them, there sweep out into the broad plain, in nearly parallel lines, three rivers.

When Lewis and Clark made their memorable expedition to the headwaters of the Missouri in 1804, and arrived at the Three Forks, it was found impossible to decide which of these three streams should be considered as the prolongation of the Missouri, and receive its name. They therefore named them after three eminent statesmen of that period, the Jefferson, the Madison, and the Gallatin. It would be hard to find a more beautiful picture of pastoral loveliness than in the vicinity of the junction of these three sparkling streams. The railroad skirts closely the right bank of the Missouri after crossing the valley and passing the "meeting of the waters."

The Upper Cañon of the Missouri is soon reached, and for twenty miles or more the scenes that greet the eye, as the train rolls through the gorge, call forth exclamations of delight from every true lover of nature.

The high walls, buttressed and chiseled on a grand scale, with crags and cliffs black and weather-beaten, develop new and unexpected figures at each turn of the cañon. Now, indeed, we are afforded a spectacle worth seeing, and the wonderful walls and beautiful river tearing along below form such a contrast to the turbid, foul stream that we saw at Bismarck, that one can hardly credit the fact that they are one and the same stream, simply under different conditions. For mile after mile the train races the noisy river, and we admire the massive walls, squared, hewed, and quarried into picturesque and robust forms, blocks, and ledges, and then turn and gaze upon some reach of swirling water more attractive than usual. After awhile the train gives it up, and shooting away from the stream, leaves it to pursue its way "unvexed to the sea."

At Helena, well named the "Queen City of the Mountains"— at least so far as the outlook from the place is concerned — a very extended view is to be had. Back of and around it rise mountains in themselves well worth a passing glance. Mount Helena is a fine old landmark, and is especially impressive viewed from the Hotel Broadwater.

To the north, west, and northeast in the foreground is a wide plain, sloping upward in billowy roughness to the mountain flanks far away, blue and sensuous. Outlined against the sky, in irregular, serrated profile, lie masses of slumberous mountains. In the distance, to the north, is seen a break, a notch through the range. This is the "Gate of the Mountains," named by Lewis and Clark; and through this cañon—a point of interest to the tourist in search of pleasure and fine scenery — the Missouri pours itself, turns toward the rising sun, and sluggishly flows to join the Father of Waters.

Helena is the capital of Montana, and is a type of the Western city. Of accidental birth, caused by the discovery of placer diggings of great richness in a gulch now become the central part of the city, it grew rapidly, and, subservient to the washing out of the placers, accommodatingly placed itself in the gulch and on the hills, so as to be out of the way as much as possible until such time as the exhausted diggings might allow it to replace itself, when, as usually happens, it was too late to rectify early blunders.

Helena is the center of an interesting mining region, the truth of which statement can be very easily verified upon inquiry, and all information needed to enable the tourist to see something of actual mining is readily obtained.

Helena's population is 15,000, or thereabouts, and it, of course, has electric lights and electric car lines, etc. Indeed, in this respect Western cities are in advance of the East.

Reader, I wonder if you have ever, like the writer, ridden for hours on horseback, during the summer solstice, over plains denuded of verdure and foliage, seared and stifling, and at last, when tired, thirsty, dusty, eyes aching, lips swollen and cracked, have reached a tiny spring at the mountain's edge, with a bit of shade and a patch of God's green earth around it, and thrown yourself down to drink and rest and be refreshed.

If so, you will understand what it was to me, when, after two days of dusty travel, I rested a day at the Broadwater Hotel. The comparison is not exactly a fair one, I admit, yet it expresses my idea, and I let it stand.

The Broadwater is a revelation, almost a dream. Placed in the midst of a park of forty acres at the foot and side of Mount Helena, with winding walks and drives, playing fountains, rippling pools, fragrant flower-beds, green lawns, and drooping foliage about them, are two large buildings in the Moorish style of architecture. One of these is the hotel proper, the other the great nata-torium. The hotel is indeed a retreat. Pleasing in exterior appearance, with an endless array of porches and balconies and towers, elegantly furnished within, with a table simply perfection, it is an experience worth having to stop there for one day, if for no more. The bedrooms are electric lighted, and supplied with water from hot springs, and heated by steam. The private baths, of which there are forty, are unusually fine, and a feature of the place. The natatorium is the largest in the world.

"The great twin-towered building is of Moorish architecture, 150 x 350 feet in size, 100 feet to the crowning roof, with towers half as high again. The roof is supported upon circular trusses, leaving the large interior entirely free from column or support that might obstruct the view. It is lighted by 20,000 square feet of colored cathedral glass by day, and a multitude of electric lamps by night. A full million gallons of hot mineral water run through it daily, half as much cold spring water being required to temper this scalding flood for the use of bathers. The hot water bubbles up through a small geyser cone, being caught in a shallow fountain-like basin, into which tumbles a sparkling cascade of cold water from a forty-foot seeming precipice of vine-entwined, moss-grown granite. The swimming pool is 100 x 300 feet in size, constructed of stone and cement, the tempered spring overflow keeping it constantly supplied with ever-changing water. It varies in depth from two to twelve feet, and is surrounded by a railed promenade ten feet in width, upon which 100 large steam-heated dressing-rooms open. A careful analysis of the water of these springs shows that they are almost identical in character with those of the celebrated hot springs of Arkansas."

Don't fail to stop and visit the Broadwater.

Leaving Helena, the main ridge of the Rockies stands athwart our course. This is crossed by means of the Mullan tunnel.

Lieut. John Mullan, U. S. A., was one of Gov. Stevens' engineers when the original survey for the Northern Pacific Railroad was made. He explored and built a wagon road across the Rocky Mountains at what is known as Mullan's Pass. It is under the summit of this pass that the tunnel is bored, and the name of the pass has *descended* to the tunnel. It is 3,850 feet long, and 5,547 above sea level.

From Helena to Spokane, a distance of nearly 400 miles, the tourist is regaled with an endless succession, and a varied one, of fine scenery. It is largely mountain, interspersed with many little mountain valleys, and some larger ones. Brawling brooks and more sedately flowing rivers are crossed and skirted.

As the train slides down the glistening rails west of the Mullan tunnel, it meanders through a park country, with fresh, green, rolling hills, devoid of the severer features of the eastern approach. All through these mountains the prospector has sunk his shafts and driven his little adits, the dumps from which can be seen more especially on the eastern slopes.

The road soon reaches an enthusiastic little river, and one noted for its varied nomenclature. It has its rise among the mountains around Butte, and is first known as Silver Bow River. When it reaches the Deer Lodge Valley it becomes the Deer Lodge River, and then successively the Hell Gate, Missoula, and Clark's Fork of the Columbia. As if this were not enough, some maps add to it the names of the Bitter Root, Cœur d'Aléne, and Pend d'Oreille. Staggering under this load of names, it is a lovely stream under each and all of them, and forms a feature of this part of the country.

The traveler first makes acquaintance with the Hell Gate, and admires its frisky ways as he watches it gamboling along. Through some fine mountain defiles, past cheery little clearings, mid prim, spinster-like tree clumps, he follows it to Missoula. The Hell Gate is of rather a vagrant disposition, roaming about in a promiscuous sort of a way.

The cañon of the Hell Gate furnishes, as intimated, some pleasant types of scenery. The gorge is not a profound one, that works the spectator up to a pitch of enthusiasm, but there are many delightful bits of cañon structure to be seen. At one or two points the cone-pointed trees, growing on the flanks of the cañon in heavy masses, produce interesting effects.

CLARK'S FORK OF THE COLUMBIA—LAKE PEND D'OREILLE.

From Missoula, Mont., one of the best cities along the entire line of the Northern Pacific, the iron horse pushes snortingly over the lofty Mission Mountains into the delectable valley of the Jocko. Some of the most attractive scenes to be found are centered in this neighborhood.

From the rippling Jocko, the parallel bands of steel wind over into the half cañon, half valley, of Clark's Fork of the Columbia. This stream is followed to Lake Pend d'Oreille.

Throughout this stretch the sightseer needs to have both eyes wide open, and be prepared to make frequent changes of position. If the rear platform of the train is available, so much the better.

At Hope, a strangely built place, the streets rising in terraces up the cliff-side, an embryo watering resort of the far Northwest is found.

Lake Pend d'Oreille will vie with pretty much anything in the category of lakes, and far surpasses many that have a wider reputation. For an outing season, where rest and pleasure, combined with sport, for the fundamental essentials, and garnished with splendid lake and mountain scenery and a rejuvenating air, I know of nothing, so easily reached, superior to this gem of a place. The man or woman in search of recreation and a surcease from confining labor or household cares, can do no better than to make Hope a center of operations, and by horse and boat explore the shoreland beauties of bay and dell, take a noonday lunch and siesta on one of the rocky islets which pop up from the glassy surface of the lake, climb about among the hills and cliffs, and return laden with the perfume of the mountains.

Only a short distance to the southward lies the sister lake, Cœur d'Aléne, very different in appearance.

A camping trip around the shores of these lakes and through the mountains lying between, will recuperate wasted bodies, steady shaky nerves, re-establish poor blood circulation, harden the muscles, and build up new tissue, so that life will seem worth the living as it never did before. Go there and try it.

THE BUTTE AIR LINE.

The traveler over the Northern Pacific who desires to see the most within a given time — and there is a wonderful sight to see between Chicago and St. Paul, and Tacoma and Portland — will find two detours from the main line that will repay the taking, either in going or returning.

The first of these is over what is known as the Butte Air Line. This is a line constructed from Logan, near the junction of the three rivers which together form the Missouri, to Butte, the great mining city, and thence, via the Montana Union Railway, to Garrison, where the main line west of Helena is again reached. This road follows at first, and for many miles, the windings of the scenic Jefferson River, a far West monument, if such it can be termed, of the third President of the United States.

Traversing its broad and pastoral valley, whose wide, well-watered plains reflect the bountiful fertility of the soil and the invigorating character of the atmosphere, until the outlying flanks of the mountains are reached, the rails begin to ascend.

Through the cañon of the Jefferson, where the hills rise in dark masses of time-browned rocks, with harsh, ugly angles, they thread their way, skimming the edges of the bluffs, plunging into savage defiles, then out again into the open. Finally the point is attained where the granite masses rise in front and on the sides, and the surmounting of the barrier must begin in earnest.

Now is seen an engineering problem worth seeing. From almost the very foot of this long circuitous ascent, a point is visible around which the track winds, which is approximately near the summit of the climb. In all directions, at all elevations, the glistening rails can be seen squirming about the sides of the hills, hanging on to the cliffs, jumping the ravines, insinuating themselves here, there, everywhere, as if determined that no place should escape that offered a projection upon which they might hang themselves in their indomitable push for the highest.

Through the Homestake tunnel, driven into the granites, the train follows its splendid track, and then the descent into the valley of the Silver Bow is begun.

For miles the roadway has been blasted out of solid granite, and the enormous cubes, shattered from their hold on the parent rocks by the powerful explosives used, lie tumbled about the mountain's side in all imaginable positions.

A scene of picturesque confusion these old granite chunks make. True to their mission to serve mankind as enduring memorials of deeds performed or virtues possessed, these, as they lie here supine, dismembered, disembodied, are lasting monuments to the power of mind over matter.

Descending these rugged, granitoid cliffs, and meandering the valley below, there is afforded a many-sided view of Butte, with its countless smelters thronging the valley, and its scores of chimneys and hoisting works perched upon every available knoll. Almost unconsciously there comes to us a paraphrase of a passage in the celebrated " Rienzi's Address to the Romans ":

> This is Butte!
> That sat on her naked hills, and from her throne
> Of silver ruled the world.

Butte has advanced to the head of all mining camps or cities of the world. Its reputation and position are ahead of that once held by the renowned Comstock Lode of Nevada. Its altitude is 5,878 feet above the sea, and its yearly output of gold, silver, lead, copper, etc., exceeds $30,000,000. It has all the appointments of an Eastern city, and those who live, or ever have lived, there, cherish for it an affection somewhat surprising to the outsider, who sees it only in a superficial way.

From Butte to Anaconda, twenty-six miles away, the road — the Montana Union — follows the cañon of the Silver Bow River, where another fine exhibition of cañon grandeur is given. Anaconda is reached by a branch from the main line, but can be seen, to the west, very plainly. It has a population of 6,000, and is as noted for its smelters as is Butte for its mines.

Leaving the cañon, the Silver Bow becomes the Deer Lodge River, and the cañon a wide, beautiful vale, fertile and prosperous, framed by mighty mountains.

THE CŒUR D'ALÉNE BRANCH LINE.

The second one of these pleasant breaks in the continuity of a long journey has for its initial point either Missoula or Spokane.

Leaving either place in the morning, the tourist, if leaving Missoula, is taken without any ado straight within the confines of a region of foaming river and precipitous and overhanging cliffs. If Spokane be the starting point, his ride for an hour or two will be over a wide-spreading plain. He then exchanges the car for a commodious, stanch, and well-appointed steamer, and steams over the limpid waters of the sleeping and restful lake ycleped Cœur d'Aléne. For five delightful hours the steamer cuts the waters of the lake and follows the windings of the Cœur d'Aléne River.

The Cœur d'Aléne Mountains are full of the precious metals which the good book says are apt to prove a curse to those who possess them. The mining interests here are great, and steadily increasing in importance.

Altogether, in its attractions industrial and scenic, the useful and ornamental, it is a locality well meriting the study and observation of the traveler.

It is difficult, ofttimes, to boldly declare that any one spot among many of great diversity of interest and appearance is superior to any or all of the others. Differences of taste and temperament occasion strange differences in likes and dislikes, as well of natural and physical things as of persons and people. It can hardly be doubted, however, that any one could make this trip and not feel that life had gained something in enjoyment for it, and would have lost something in the missing of it. The rugged mountain scenery is of the finest along the railroad; the ride down or up the sluggish stream, with an infinitude of charming and changing vista, and across the bosom of a lake plumped down amidst kindly mountain slopes, is a welcome change.

Like all else in mundane affairs, any one sort of scenic attraction becomes monotonous if long continued. The flat plain absolutely tires one after a spell; winding river and grassy vale lose their power to charm; mountain and cliff, no matter how inspiring they may at first have been, may, by the very supremity of their grandeur and effect, so exhaust the power to appreciate that, sated and wearied with the tremendous draught upon the senses, the mind turns from them, utterly exhausted.

Just at this point this lake and river ride comes in to refresh and enliven man's tired nature.

Plains and rivers he has seen galore, and mountains have risen before him in lofty profile and dignified hauteur. Now comes this bit of a change — for the lake itself, while mountain walled, is not dominated by the haughty, stern, uncompromising peaks one might imagine. The rather, they are soft-browed, low-lying, and gentle in aspect, and the hither slopes daintily rounded by the rains and melting snows from heaven. Like as it were the benediction after a sermon which has held the listener spellbound, with nerves keyed to the highest pitch; like the glowing sunset after the equinoctial storm, it glides softly in upon us, and we glide softly in and upon it, feeling a peace, a rest, a tranquillity of spirit, refreshing and calming.

By all means, let all who can spare the time enjoy the voyage of the twain Cœur d'Alénes, lake and river.

CROSSING THE CASCADE RANGE.

"Westward the course of Empire takes its way," and we follow in its trail.

Spokane, the metropolis of Eastern Washington, is a city the entire State of Washington is proud of. And well may she be. Admirably located at the Falls of the Spokane, a water-power of both great beauty and utility, well laid out, cleanly, with noble buildings, a people of push and energy, boasting some

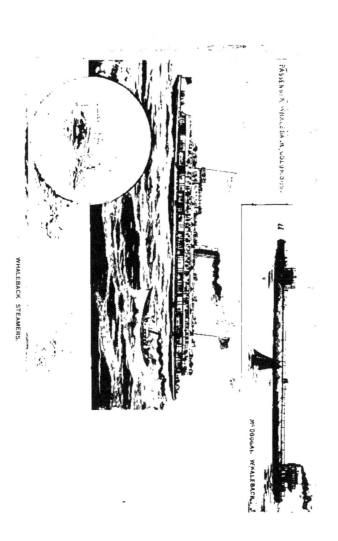

PASSENGER WHALEBACK, COLUMBUS

WHALEBACK STEAMERS.

MC DOUGAL WHALEBACK.

NORTH DAKOTA WHEAT FIELDS.

of the most elegant private grounds of any city in the United States, it may well be considered an index of the future prosperity of the country tributary to it. It has emerged from the ruin wrought by its great fire some years since, improved and purified, and on the whole, every whit the better for it.

Leaving Spokane, the railroad sweeps to the southwest across an elevated, basaltic plain to the crossing of the mighty Columbia, that writhing serpent of water, whose eddying rapids and ugly rocks make of it a failure for long and continuous navigation.

Swinging now to the west and northwest, the train rolls through the valleys of the Yakima and Kittitas and the Yakima Cañon. Far and wide extends the reputation of these valleys in the Pacific Coast country for their fruitfulness and stock-raising qualities.

Leaving these to the rear, we near the crowning feature of the long, long journey — the passage of the Cascades.

The glory of the Cascades is that, unlike the Rockies, they push their pine-decked flanks and stormy summits straight from old ocean's level up thousands of feet into the cold, azure vault above. Here the effect of prodigious mountain masses is realized to an extent impossible in the Rocky Range. To the person who has seen mountains only as exemplified in the Appalachian system, the Alleghenies, the Adirondacks, the Blue Ridge, the White Mountains of the East, the sensation is exciting, the revelation a surprising one.

Slowly the long train drags up the curving incline, pulled by two massive locomotives. Above us the steep sides tower, thickly covered with "the forest primeval"; below, they plunge down into the wild glens and tangled ravines.

When we make the last stop previous to entering the Stampede tunnel, I hasten forward and seat myself in the cab of the monster helper locomotive in the lead. Perched between the mammoth boiler and the cab window I am ready for the next move.

They are working in the great boring, but at last the signal comes, and away we go. Rounding a curve, the black mouth of the tunnel swings into sight. On each side of us, as we whirl along, are side tracks filled with construction trains. High overhead, above the tunnel, rises the mountain, and plunging down its rocky face comes a beautiful cascade.

With accelerated speed we rush into the darkness, and the exhaust of the locomotives and the noise of the train are fairly bewildering at first. Then we see that the tunnel is lighted by electric lights. Some of the lights are on a line low down on the side of the tunnel, some are up near the roof. For a long distance ahead we can see them, faint and red. The effect is weird and peculiar, like a long line of indistinct stars gazed at through smoked glass. When daylight is again found we are on the other side of the summit. The helper is here disconnected from the train, and I climb up into the cab of the other engine for a ride down the mountains. I had taken the precaution to obtain a written permit giving me the privilege of locomotive riding at any time, a procedure rendered necessary by the rules of the operating department in this regard.   My credentials not only allowed me the freedom of the engine, but induced the engineer to place me on his seat behind him where he could point out to me the objects of interest.

It was twilight when the ride down the mountain began.   The sun had drifted out of sight behind the labyrinth of peaks, the *confrères* of Mount Tacoma farther to the west.   No "curfew tolled the knell of parting day," no "lowing herd wound slowly o'er the lea"; but the soft calm of evening, and evening amidst surroundings the most uplifting, was there, and the world was rapidly being left "to darkness and to me."

At the point where the passage of the range is effected, a network of gorges head, radiating westwardly in many directions.   These cañons or gorges, as you please, are deep, their sides very steep, and they are covered with a dense growth of coniferous trees.   Between these profound ravines the mountains throw out more or less lengthy and abrupt points or spurs, and it is along the sides of these, and around their terminal fronts, that the railroad cleaves its pathway.   As it starts at the summit, it is of course higher above the bottoms of the gorges, but is far below the crest lines of the ridges and heights.

Opening the throttle-valve, enough steam is turned on to simply give the heavy train a good start down the grade.   Then the steam is shut off and we go thundering along, borne onward by that powerful, unseen force the discovery of which immortalized the name of Sir Isaac Newton.

With increasing speed we skim along the narrow pathway scraped out of the mountain side.   Faster and faster turn the driving-wheels, louder grows the roar of the train; the engine sways and rocks from side to side, and jolts upon her heavy springs, as she warms to her work.   Now the end of the first spur is reached, and we seem as if about to leap far out into the yawning gulf which opens before us.   The mighty engine, trembling in every fiber, inclines to one side, and taking the sharp curve, away we shoot around the promontory, and then go sweeping back on our course along the opposite side of the spur.   Far above us lies the old switchback which for years did duty while the Stampede tunnel was being driven, and is now being torn up, its day of usefulness gone. Above us still, but below the switchback, we trace the iron pathway along which we have but just been flying.   Ahead of us, climbing up a dizzy height, opens an avenue cleft through the black forest.   It marks the line of the tunnel.   As a few moments before we seemed bent on plunging into eternity, so now we seem to be driving straight at the wall of mountain which rises solidly ahead of us.   Again inclining herself, the bounding machine under us follows the graceful track as it bends to the curvature of the mountain, and circling around the head of a ravine we are once more sailing along the side of another cliff-like slope.   Thus we go for mile after mile in a thrilling, exciting race. It seems time and again as if naught could hold and check the rushing thing upon which we ride; but with hand upon the air-brake lever the engineer controls the impatient machine as deftly and easily as a mother her romping child. Not once during the ride down the grade are the brakes of the train wholly freed from their clutch on the wheels. When the speed is a little more than is right, an extra turn of the little brass handle and the wheels are gripped a little harder and the momentum checked.

As we went sweeping along through the ever-shifting scenes about us, cutting the keen sides of the mountains, thundering over bridges, shooting through cuts, waltzing around points, I had my first view of Mount Tacoma. Touching me on the arm the engineer pointed out the peak to me. From that point of view it is nothing like the magnificent spectacle it is when viewed from a good point forty or fifty miles away. As I turned my gaze toward it, it was with a feeling of deepest awe and respect for the old monarch. " Every inch a king," with his white ægis wrapped about him; cold, haughty, solemn, he looks down with a noble dignity on the lesser peaks which rise about him — satellites to the greater, the master.

At Weston, the first stop after leaving the tunnel, the traveler is often treated to an unusual and dramatic sight in railroading.

As the train turns the abrupt bluff just before reaching Weston, far below it, runs a wooded gulch, stretching away in the distance, a rich, enduring picture. It is the valley and cañon of the Green River, one of the most attractive, and finest trout-fishing streams of the Pacific Coast. At Weston the westbound train takes the side track for the eastbound train to pass.

. Just beyond the switch stand the track turns in a beautiful curve, crosses the purling stream, and swings back parallel to, and some distance under, the track at the station and beyond, as it rounds the bluff before named. Usually we have here the unique and very interesting spectacle of two trains, one bound toward the rising the other toward the setting sun, and both for a time running parallel to each other and in the same direction.

Upon this particular night the Eastern train was behind time. So soon as it passed us the engineer, who wished me to see the sight presented, pulled out. The train quickly acquired its usual speed, but when a point was reached where the other train should be visible, it was not in sight. Giving the throttle an extra jerk the puffing monster responded with a vim, and we went tearing down the grade trying to beat old Time. I put my head out the cab window and watched the train as it swung around the curve at increasing speed. The effort failed. The other train was not caught that night. Upon my return trip I saw what on this occasion I missed. I remained on the locomotive until late, and saw the highly picturesque scenery of the tortuous, narrow cañon of the Green, lighted up by the headlight of the engine. It was a thoroughly weird and novel ride, and a wild one.

THE KOOTENAI COUNTRY.

WHERE IT IS—

ITS CHARACTERISTICS.

UST north of the boundary line between the United States and British Columbia, in about longitude 117°, lies a mountain range which, within the last few years, has become noted for the magnificence of its scenery.

The southern end of this range is in the midst of a region which, once it becomes well known to the enterprising tourist, will become the Mecca of many a pilgrimage.

A hundred miles to the east of the Selkirks rise the massive peaks of the Rockies, reaching in this latitude their greatest development. Upon the western slope of this range are gathered the headwaters of two large rivers. Fed by the same snows which in the autumn and winter months cover the crests and gorges of the range in whitened splendor, their farthest threads of drainage trickling from snow fields in near proximity to each other, they yet begin their journeys to the sea flowing in opposite directions; both wind about and among lowering mountains, expand into deep, long, and beautiful lakes, and then, as if overjoyed at again drawing near together, throw themselves into each other's embraces in a frenzy of joy and rapture.

From its sources here, the historic Columbia flows away northward, gouges its way through the Selkirks, and then turns back upon itself, and after swelling out into the long and narrow Arrow Lakes — after the fashion of the Mississippi River at Lake Pepin — it wends its way in rapid current, amidst lusty mountain scenery, into United States territory and to the sea. Likewise, the scarcely less interesting Kootenai River flows southward between the Rockies on the east and the Purcell Range on the west, down for some distance into the limits of Montana. Here it also wheels upon itself, and flows across a corner of Idaho back into British Columbia. A short distance above the boundary it expands into the three-armed Kootenai Lake, leaving which it meanders in a southwesterly direction to its union with the Columbia.

From the point where it leaves the lake to its junction with the Columbia, a distance of between twenty-five and thirty miles, it affords one of the finest specimens of river scenery to be found on the continent. It is a fitting

YELLOWSTONE R.

YELLOWSTONE RIVER.

HOTEL BROADWATER AND NATATORIUM.

valedictory to the career of varied and charming scenic effects which has preceded it.

To gain entrance to this land of delight and pleasure, the best route is to leave the Northern Pacific road at Spokane, taking the Spokane & Northern Railway to its northern terminus at Northport, Wash. At this point a steamer is in waiting for the sixty-mile ride up the swift-flowing Columbia to Robson. Here the Columbia & Kootenai Railroad is taken for the ride up the banks of the Kootenai River and for the Kootenai Lake trip. (If the Arrow Lakes be the objective point, the journey by steamer will be continued.) This route to be used also on the return trip.

The Kootenai region is valuable in but two ways. One is as a scenic and health resort, the other as a promising mining center. As an agricultural or pastoral section it is valueless. Some day the forests of the Selkirks may to some extent have a commercial value.

In a mining sense the region becomes more important every year. New towns on both sides of the lake are being built up, new mining camps and centers established. At Ainsworth and Kaslo, on the west side of the lake, many and good mines are being developed. At Pilot Bay, on the eastern side, a fine smelter is in process of construction. Nelson, the largest town in the locality, is situated on the southern shore of the west arm of the lake, and is an outfitting point for the surrounding country.

In the Ainsworth group of mines the ores are largely composed of galena, varying from 20 per cent to 70 per cent of lead, and very rich in silver. One peculiarity here is that the higher the mine the richer it is. The lower grade ores are in the mines at lower elevations, and high grade ores are found where the mines are high up on the mountains. The Sky Line mine, back of Ainsworth, 4,000 feet above the lake, and the now celebrated Silver King mine on Toad Mountain, near Nelson, are examples of this. The latter mine was estimated to have, in the summer of 1892, a half million dollars worth of ore on the dump.

North of Nelson, and up in the mountains, and also west of Kaslo, is the new Slocan district. This has created much excitement on account of the apparent richness of the region. As yet, the camp is so young that definite predictions as to the value of deposits other than near the surface can not be made, but the prospects, according to those who know, are of the best.

If the value of the Kootenai country as a mineral region becomes as sure as it is from a scenic point of view, between the two the world will soon become much better acquainted with it.

KOOTENAI LAKE.

Upon the old maps of the country Kootenai Lake is laid down as Flat Bow Lake. This may have been the translation of an Indian name for the lake, but however this may be, the present name, given it presumably from the tribe of Indians who frequent the region has been for years and is now the name universally used.

Like most Indian names there are several spellings of the word. The British Columbians use the form Kootenay, and we of this side the line seem to prefer Kootenai. The spellings Kootenaie and Coo-too-nay have also been used, but in general use are now practically obsolete.

This enchanting sheet of water occupies a longitudinal depression or valley, long and narrow, between the Selkirk Range on the west and the Purcells — apparently a part of the Rocky Mountains — on the east. In the absence of trustworthy official surveys and accurate maps it is difficult to state many points with exactitude. The maps show an Upper and a Lower Kootenai Lake, the upper lake being but a small one, and some fifteen miles or more north of the main lake.

Kootenai Lake proper is an expansion of the Kootenai River, and is variously stated to be from sixty-five to ninety miles in length, and of a remarkably even width of about three miles, and a depth of 400 feet. The western arm of the lake as it is usually termed, but what would really seem to be more correctly called again, the Kootenai River, leaves the lake proper very near the middle of the west shore and flows somewhat south of west to Nelson, a distance of about twenty miles. Here the name of the river does again assert itself for the remainder of its career of twenty-five or thirty miles to its uniting with the Columbia.

It would seem that the lake might with propriety be divided into three parts for convenience sake, and these designations really mean something. What is now known as the upper lake is so remote from the larger one, and so small, that a new name might much better be given it. At the place where the western arm leads out there is a slight stricture and flexure in the lake, and the northern arm, counting from this point, is both longer and somewhat wider, than the southern member. One, therefore, hearing the terms Upper and Lower Lake naturally associates them with these two sections of the main lake, and I shall accordingly so refer to them.

It is authoritatively stated that the lake once extended far southward up the Kootenai Valley from its present lower limit, and that the filling up of the valley by the debris brought down by the river has contracted it. It is not hard to credit this, for the banks of the river are low, and draining an extensive mountain area as it does, the vernal floods must bring down an immense amount of fertilizing material, which is spread abroad o'er the wide valley. The Kootenai River valley is from three to five miles wide, and these annual freshets are said to convert the whole lower valley into an immense temporary lake. A great reclamation scheme has been devised, which if carried to successful completion will bring under cultivation nearly 50,000 acres of the finest of bottom lands, the greater portion of which will be within the limits of the United States.

Leaving Bonner's Ferry at 3 o'clock A. M. the steamer has nearly reached the foot of the lake before its passengers are on deck. As the steamer glides past a large island and issues forth into the lake, freed from obstructing bends and banks, the scene is one of great loveliness. Instead of stupendous mountains hemming us in, making us feel as if we were navigating within the bowels of the earth, the hills and mountains seem of the diminutive sort, and gently pleasing in outline, and the view and feeling at first is one of peace and quiet. As the river and its low shores are left farther and farther to the rear, and we plow our frothy way nearer to the center of the lake, the panorama changes. Gradually the mountains on the western side, which lie back from the shore and are at first hidden from view, show themselves, rising tier above tier. A little more rugged, somewhat more angular and fierce they become as they come to the front and are nearer to the heart of the range. And everywhere they are shaggy with forests. Still onward we go, the water growing deeper with each boat length that we advance, and the color becoming of a more lake-like, beryl hue. Our course is through the middle of the watery plain, midway between the mountained shores. After some miles of progress the scene is one inspiring, imposing, exalting.

A vast prairie, not of gracefully bending grasses, but of dancing, shining water, encompasses us. To front and rear it stretches in level quiet, save in our wake, where the foam-flecked swells and wavelets, glittering in the morning sun, break the lazy monotony. At each side it reaches out toward the high, unyielding walls which mark its confines, and which, though speechless, say in unmistakable tones, "Thus far and no farther."

Bounding the laken plain the mountain heights now rise to great altitudes, and as they run to the north, higher and yet higher they grow. The scene of calm and peace is still with us, but withal of such added sternness, might, dignity, and grandeur, as to entirely alter the aspect. The sun strikes the western range and reveals the rugged slopes in all their detail, while the Purcells stand out, apparently not so deeply seamed and wrinkled, and more gentle in contour, and of longer and less broken slopes.

Almost midway of the entire lake, and opposite the western arm, is a picturesque, shore-wooded inlet known as Pilot Bay. Here a stop is made for a few minutes, and then the steamer's prow turns northward, and we are cutting the waters of the Upper Lake. The scenery from this point onward is much finer than any heretofore seen. A long and lovely stretch of water lies ahead; the mountains break down on the west shore and disclose the water-gap whence issues the western arm; the lake here is wider than below, and the array of mountains is on a much grander scale. Far ahead they rise on either side of the water in sharp, angry peaks and cañon-cleft slopes on the one side, and in sweeping, longitudinal masses of long and lofty curvature on the other. Nearer at hand the cañons and gorges which eat back into the heart of the Selkirks can be seen, and some idea gained of the rough and wild character of its scenic features once its inner recesses are penetrated. As the range retreats from the lake it becomes more wild and rugged, and reaches at its culminating points elevations of 8,000 and 9,000 feet above the sea. At a point from the center of the lake, opposite Ainsworth, the view is probably, on the whole, the finest to be had. Here the expanse of lake itself visible is perhaps the most extensive, while the mountains rise in more massive folds, and present a landscape wonderfully fine and stately in its *tout ensemble*. With its tremendous terraces, bristling peaks, great ridges and crest lines, and magnificent slopes, canopied thickly with pines, spruces, cedars, balsams, and dappled in the higher parts with gleaming snow-banks, it presents a cycloramic picture of sharply contrasted mountain and lake seldom equaled, let alone surpassed. The distant perspective to the north is especially fine. There the mountains are built on a colossal plan, and thrust high above timber line into the realm of perpetual snow, sharp, angular, bald points, about which the cold blasts whistle, the storm cloud nestles, and along whose keen sides the snow-flake finds lodgment. The domain of King Boreas this, and few there be of the human kind who will care to invade his dominions.

Through the tangled labyrinth of virgin forest, back in the heart of the Selkirks especially, twisting water channels of foamy cascade, swirling brook, and leaping torrent wend their noisy way to the lake. Beautiful lakes, not only of purest water, but of ice opaline in hue; enormous snow-fields, flowing in frozen falls over cliffs; glaciers enthroned among the cold, gray, austere crags, will well repay the hardy adventurer's tramp afoot among the wild fastnesses of the range. Severe and arduous as it is plunging through underbrush and fallen timber, threading trackless wilds — for trails there are none, climbing over the bowlders which mark the path of the snow-slide, there is a fascination in it that never grows less, and which spurs the daring one on to attempt fresh difficulties; to climb where it would appear that only goats could penetrate.

The shores of the lake abound in romantic spots, high bluffs, pleasant beaches. The waters and streams are full of trout that can be had for the casting of the line. The lover of nature and the fisherman can each find all the employment they desire.

BUTTE CITY, MONTANA.

STEAMER GEORGE GATES.

CŒUR D'ALENE RIVER.

CŒUR D'ALENE LAKE AND RIVER.

THE BIG BEND AND THE PALOUSE REGIONS.

THE BIG BEND COUNTRY.

HE city of Spokane is located in the midst of a region which is certain to support in the future a very large population. A glance at the map will show that the Northern Pacific Railroad and its branches spread out antennæ-like in all directions from this common center.

From the east, and to the west, runs the main line of road — a great trunk and thoroughfare from coast to coast. To the southeast is the Cœur d'Aléne branch, tapping the treasures of the Cœur d'Aléne mines. To the south runs a line into the celebrated Palouse country, a region of wonderful fecundity. The stories told of wheat crops here, and authentic too, almost stagger one's credulity.

To the north the Spokane & Northern Railroad, whose relations with the Northern Pacific are close and friendly, traverses the glorious Colville Valley, to the Columbia River and the Kootenai country.

To the west the Central Washington branch of the Northern Pacific extends to Coulée City, and the country penetrated by this road is one of the most remarkable known in the West.

After entering the United States the Columbia River flows in a general southerly direction for more than a hundred miles. Its course for this distance is almost entirely inclosed by mountains. When the comparatively open country is reached, the river commits one of those apparently inconsistent, capricious acts so common to western water-ways. Instead of seeking the land of sunshine it petulantly wheels to the west-northwest, and clings closely to the mountain country. This course it maintains for another hundred miles as the river runs. Sweeping then in long, winding reaches to the southwest, south, and southeast, it swings back in the vicinity of Pasco to the longitude from which it began this eccentric career. The Northern Pacific Railroad, from Spokane to Pasco, virtually forms the chord of which the Columbia is the arc, and between this arc and its chord is an upland region known as the Big Bend country.

This section constitutes one of Nature's paradoxes. On the old maps this is noted as the great plain of the Columbia. Both axes of this plain are about one hundred and fifty miles in length. Its surface is broken and rolling, largely denuded of trees, scantily watered, and ranges from 1,000 to 3,000 feet above sea level. It is not devoid of interesting physical features.

In the long ago it has been the scene of extensive volcanic disturbance, and the basaltic monuments of this period are scattered far and wide. Two extensive couleés or cañons wind over the region, with vertical walls of basalt, in places many hundreds of feet in height. These are known as the Grand Coulée and Moses Coulée. Basaltic ledges and domes, some of them very striking or picturesque, dot the land. At Coulée City, the present western terminus of the Central Washington branch, the exposure of basalt cliffs forming the western side of the Grand Coulée is exceptionally fine. Hundreds of feet in elevation, its swarthy cliffs extend for several miles without sign of break, and are visible for a long distance; a most imposing mural sight.

From Coulée City numerous stage lines extend across this country in different directions into the mountain and mining districts upon its northern and western borders. To the north lies the Okanogan region, rapidly growing in importance both as a mining and stock-raising center. During the first part of the present century the Hudson Bay Company and the Northwest Fur Company had rival posts in this section when the fur trade was at its best. Its fastnesses were penetrated in those days by the *voyageur* and trader seeking after peltries, and by the missionary seeking after the souls of the Indians. The spirit of the times has changed. Instead of the wandering trapper setting his traps in the icy streams, the ubiquitous prospector is seen climbing the hills, scrambling up the gulches, blasting and tunneling into the mountains, searching out the hidden treasures of the divine alchemist.

In riding over the Big Bend region one is first struck by the contradictory character of things. The whole extent of it, judging from surface appearances, is absolutely worthless, barring a few alluvial spots here and there. The grayish white soil, seemingly of an alkaline nature, appears sterile enough, and to have little depth. The absence of trees and the presence of basaltic ledges, and the small fragments of the same scattered about, intensify this conclusion. The great scarcity of running streams simply compels such belief.

After riding for a few miles with this fact gradually and finally forced upon one, he is somewhat startled upon rounding a curve of the road or ascending a hill to find at one side of the road and perched upon the summit, one of the finest wheat fields he ever saw, and on the opposite side the same dreary stretch of monotonous land heretofore seen. He wonders what it means. Soon the same phenomenon is again presented, with the exception that instead of a grain field it is a tremendous potato patch. Again, from an elevated piece of road he will obtain an extensive view of an entire farm. Hillock and hollow are covered with luxuriant, yellow fields of standing grain waiting for the reaper to gather it in. Meadows fresh and green are in effective contrast with the golden fields on one side, the dull, unbroken prairie on the other. A comfortable house surrounded by fields of vegetables equal to any to be found elsewhere, and with well and out-buildings, completes the chain of evidence that the land is, after all, of some account. By the time one has ridden over this region in many directions for two or three hundreds of miles, and seen this in endless repetition, he will conclude, as did I, that it is the old story of the singed cat over again—that the country is a vast deal better than it looks. This feeling is specially enforced by the wonderful color of everything seen. No sickly, uncertain green, but grain, potatoes, garden truck, are of the healthiest, deepest green imaginable. Therefore I say that this is "a region which is certain to support in the future a very considerable population."

The country has had a goodly number of settlers come in since the building of the railroad, but there is room for multitudes yet. Some parts of it have timber patches sufficient for fuel, corrals, etc. Good crops are raised, whether of grain, vegetables, or fruits. Water they get in wells, and I suspect there is what is known in the West as sub-irrigation available here, which provides both wells and moisture for crops. Certainly no better looking crops can be found anywhere. There was much new breaking to be seen, and the general appearance of farms, ranches, and people indicated prosperity.

THE PALOUSE COUNTRY.

South of Spokane, between the main line of the Northern Pacific Railroad on the west, the Spokane & Palouse branch line on the east, and the Snake River on the south, is the celebrated Palouse country.

It is a region of rolling, hilly prairie, some 50 x 100 miles in extent, and watered by the Palouse River and its tributaries. The greater portion of this tract is within the State of Washington; some of it, however, extends across the line into Idaho.

The Palouse River has its sources in the Cœur d'Aléne Mountains, flows for 150 miles in a general southwestern direction, and empties into the Snake River.

The surface of the Palouse country is a succession of hills and ridges covered with grass and wild sunflowers and lupins. The soil is a decomposed basalt, very rich in the ingredients that go to the making of all the small grains. Curiously enough the hill slopes and summits have not been washed of their fertility for the benefit of the valleys. On the contrary, they are just as rich as the depressions between them. There is no timber, except a few scattered pines on the hill slopes along the creeks, until you get back to the foot-hills of the mountains, which are covered with Rocky Mountain pine, fir, and tamarack.

The climate is as agreeable and healthful, taking the year round, as can be found anywhere in the United States. A short winter with moderate snowfall is followed by an early spring, beginning usually in February. In March the flowers are blooming and the plows going. There are usually three or four short hot spells in summer, but in those spells the nights are cool enough to make blankets requisite, and the rest of the summer is breezy and comfortable. In the hottest days you do not feel the heat if you are in the shade. It appears that only the sun's rays are hot, and that the air does not get heated up after the coolness of the night.

One of the peculiarities of the climate of this whole scope of country is the light rainfall and, a seeming paradox, the wonderful crops produced. The phenomenon, though, is not difficult of explanation.

The Columbia River channel furnishes a trough up which sweep the warm and moisture-laden currents from the ocean. Debouching upon the plains east of the Columbia, these vaporous currents spread themselves over a vast extent of country. At night condensation takes place, and a fine mist descends upon tree and shrub, stalk and leaf, pasture and field, furnishing through a copious dew the moisture necessary to produce the great crops. Thus it is that with no rain to speak of from May or June to October, and with an annual rainfall of about twenty inches, the soil makes such returns to the thrifty farmer. The general elevation of the region is somewhat less than 2,000 feet above the sea.

The statements of crops yielded in this Palouse Valley would seem simply untruthful were they not beyond dispute. To the farmer who is satisfied in the East with obtaining an average of from twelve to eighteen or, perhaps, twenty bushels of wheat per acre, an average crop of twenty-five to forty bushels, with frequently fifty and sixty bushels per acre, seems impossible; yet these figures are not exaggerations. Barley and oats will run from forty to sixty bushels; flax, fifteen and twenty bushels per acre. Root crops produce enormously. Apples grow well, and the more delicate fruits can be raised in the warm valleys.

Good lands here cost money. No wild land of good quality can be bought for less than $20 per acre. The purchaser, however, gets his money's worth not alone in land.

Good towns are scattered through the Palouse section and railroad facilities are much better than one has really a right to hope for. The country has settled up rapidly since the railroad entered it, and the farmers are becoming independently well off.

LAKE CHELAN.

ITS GENERAL CHARACTERISTICS.

F MOUNTAIN lakes there seems to be no end. It matters not where, among the Alpine solitudes of the far West especially, the hardy mountaineer climbs, he continually stumbles upon these exquisites of mountain travel. Literally, of tiny, sleeping lakelets there *is* no end. But of the larger class of mountain lakes, that deserve and will retain for one reason or another the affection of the traveling public, there are but few. And of these the Northwest seems to contain the most of them.

Lake Tahoe, that gem of Sierran scenery, and justly noted for great beauty, for years held undisputed the scepter for queenly pre-eminence in this regard. It can do this in all fairness no longer. Without entering into invidious comparisons, there are at least six of this class of lakes that will rival each other, both for their scenic features and piscatorial delights, It is a noteworthy fact that five of them either lie immediately along the line of or are reached from the Northern Pacific Railroad.

These six are the before-named Tahoe, lying farthest to the south; the three-armed Kootenai, at the extreme north; Yellowstone Lake — that remarkable body of water, nearly 8,000 feet above sea level — in the now famous Yellowstone National Park; Cœur d'Aléne; Pend d'Oreille, having the most sensuous. Italian-like aspect of any of them, and Lake Chelan, destined to lead them each and all, in the minds of many, in the future.

Situated at the base and under the shadow of the high Cascades, in Eastern Washington, until recently Chelan has been so remote from the highways of travel as to be scarcely known. It lies just beyond the Big Bend country, being separated from it by the Columbia River. It drains into the Columbia by the Chelan River, some three miles long, the scenery of which is one of the features of the locality. For the upper part of its course the river bowls along over a rocky bottom, flirting and dancing, apparently as happy and unconcerned as the day is long. Then it reaches the cañon, which is short, narrow, several hundred feet in elevation, and very tortuous. Through this the rampageous stream thunders in an avalanche of cascades, falls, and rapids. It is almost one continual mass of foam and spray, and no matter from what point viewed, from the road above or the edge of the water in the cañon, the sight is a beautiful one. At the mouth of the cañon, where it plunges down to the bottom-lands bordering the Columbia, it goes frisking and leaping over the rocks in a series of enchan.'ng cascades, known as the Chelan Falls. Whoever will take the short trip to this point and climb up to the shelving rocks which command the view of tus cascades, and into the pretty little cañon, will be repaid by a "water color" of refreshing interest. The value of this stream for water-power purposes will be understood when it is stated that within the short three miles of its course the fall is 300 feet.

Lake Chelan is about seventy miles in length and from two to four miles wide. It is one of the deepest lakes in the United States or, for that matter, in the world. During the year 1892 the United States Geological Survey sounded it to a depth of nearly 1,200 feet *without* reaching bottom. How much deeper than this it may be, of course can now only be conjectured.

Lake Tahoe has heretofore ranked as the deepest lake in the United States, averaging from 1,200 to 1,400 feet, with a greatest depth of 1,645 feet. Of European lakes there are but two deeper than Tahoe, viz., Lago Maggiore and Lago di Como, in Italy. It will thus be seen that Chelan is one of the few deepest lakes of the world, and future soundings may serve to place it at the head of the list, in our own country at least.

The lake is fed by numerous streams and springs which have their sources up in the great snow-fields and glaciers of the Cascade and Methow ranges. Its largest affluent is the Stehekin River at the extreme northern end of the lake, which flows down through a magnificent mountain gorge with the speed of a mill race.

One of the greatest charms of this charming inland sea is the color and transparency of the water. The color approaches closely if not quite to an ultramarine blue, and it is a pleasure simply to look at it. When very clear, one can gaze far down into its glorious depths and see the trout darting about, or discern, perhaps, a perfect labyrinth of logs and old trees, blown to the spot by the wind, and becoming waterlogged, have sunk and settled in interlocking embrace.

From the foot of the lake the view extends for twelve miles, when the mountains force a bend in the lake almost at right angles. This course then continues for several miles with increasingly fine scenery, when another change in direction is made. The general course is then much the same, the deviations being less than before. After the second deflection the scenic features are rapidly augmented, and the upper thirty-five or forty miles of the lake are, beyond all question probably, the finest mountain-girt stretch of inland lake to be seen in this country.

The first view of the lake from the lower end at Lakeside is apt to be disappointing. The domes and bluffs and crags we came to see are not here. The mountain giants, overhanging cliffs, cloud-wrapped peaks, in a word, the stupendous handiwork of the Almighty, which we were led to expect, is wanting.

From our hotel the eastern shore greets our gaze. Low, undulating, unwooded, the hills, fashioned by the waves which once lapped them, and of their kind perfect, seem at first glance flat and tame.

From many previous experiences I have learned that Nature is prone to conceal her choicest things, and require from him who would see them in their perfection some degree of patience and perseverance over difficulties, in their pursuit. The most beautiful of cañons, I once encamped before, almost within, its glowing portals, and for an entire day could see nothing of it. Wrapped and shrouded within impenetrable vapor, its speechless glories lay unrevealed to my gaze. Remembering this, I cultivate the patience required and — wait.

ON THE BOSOM OF THE WATERS.

Once out on the surface of the waters, as the steamer moves up the lake the aspect of things changes for the better. The mountains and hills rise in gentle, rounded, low terraces, with beach spots, and tree clumps, and park spots to break the monotony. Some day not far in the future, the vine and fruit tree will cover the hollows and hillocks now devoted to pasturage or grain fields.

After the steamer makes the first turn of the lake, the mountains on the west bank, which have been increasing in height, are now found rising high above the water, and of imposing and precipitous flanks. At one place there has evidently been a rock and land slide of tremendous extent. A huge mass of mountain far up at the summit has pitched forward and downward, leaving a sheer, ruddy precipice to mark the catastrophe.

After a few miles, the lake again turns somewhat to the left, and a view of much greater extent stretches before us. It is as well a sight of great power and grandeur, which is rapidly intensified as we get farther within the realm of the mountain god. Ahead of us are the narrows, where the mighty Titans, coming closer together as if determined to fall upon each other in battle royal, confine the waters within more restricted limits. Now the snowy peaks come into view in the distance. At Twenty-five Mile Creek the old hills fall back a bit and leave a large circular opening of bench and cañon; a beautiful spot.

On the other shore, Safety Harbor, a sheltering nook as its name implies, is a point of interest in this part of the lake. It is formed by a receding shore just around a monster bluff, and a little depression, half valley, half cañon, winds gently back into the Methow Range.

Up to the time that Twenty-five Mile Creek and Safety Harbor are reached, the scenic features, while fine, have not been superior. The eastern

side of the lake has had a severe struggle to reach that point where it can
with propriety deserve the name mountainous. The other side has contin-
uously grown in stature, but there has been much to see which derogated
from the severely classical mountain structure. The gaps in the range, the
open savannahs, the scantily wooded terraces, with the houses of the ranch
people strikingly placed by the shore, or back amid vistas of wild woodland,
have all served to check the evolution, or at least the effect of it, of the
overpowering mountain wall.

There now comes a great change. The bounds of this inland sea are
choked in. The low, diminutive hills vanish. The little table-lands and their
woodland homes are behind us. At the narrows a mighty transformation
takes place. The deep, blue waters, hitherto as unruffled as a fair lady's
cheek, now fret and chafe, half ripple, half wavelet, at the unwonted confine-
ment. The wind, before this quiescent, now comes hurtling down from the
Alpine snows and crags far ahead.

But look at the mountains! What mighty hand hath wrought that which
now looms up in such colossal grandeur? Upon whichever side we gaze the
same picture of stupendous heights, gigantic domes, lofty precipices, all carved
and fluted with ravines and cañons. It is a vision of terrestrial magnificence
bursting forth unexpectedly, and with awe and reverence the spectator
unconsciously feels, even though he may not utter it, "Great and marvelous
are thy works, Lord God Almighty."

It has been well said, that "There is no more beautiful or pure sheet of
water in the world, and the scenery along its banks and precipitous walls
rivals that of Switzerland, which many Americans annually cross the waters to
view and extol. As you approach the head, mountains rise right out of the
lake and seemingly pierce the skies; and when the lake is still, the reflections
in the same form pictures which, if placed on canvas, would seem greatly over-
drawn and unreal to those who had never feasted their eyes on such a sublime
spectacle. The reflections of the timbered mountains and snow-capped peaks
are just as positive as the mountains and peaks themselves."

Slowly, shall I write, with temerity, the mite of a boat rides onward, farther
and nearer — is it a paradox — into the heart of the vale of waters. It seems
to feel that it is penetrating the sacred precincts of another world. Surely this
is a Holy of Holies, and we may expect momentarily to be called upon in fear
and trembling to account to an offended majesty for this great profanation.

But not so! No avenging deity appears, and we give ourselves up to
enjoy and absorb the glorious handiwork of Him who lives in house not made
with hands, eternal in the heavens.

At numerous points cascades are seen, principally on the western side. I
fancy that in the early summer, when the heavy snows are melting rapidly, is
really the time to see Chelan in all its glory. Besides the fact that the grasses

NORTHERN PACIFIC SLEEPING CAR.

NORTHERN PACIFIC DINING CAR.

and foliage are then at their best, that mountain flowers bedeck the slopes, I know from the many dry water channels seen that the number of beautiful cascades and falls is large. For hundreds of feet they can then be seen leaping in headlong flight from the ledges above to the deep waters below.

Round Mountain is one of the interesting spots on the lake. It is a bare, brown, and weathered bluff, rising several hundred feet as an imposing precipice. Viewed from out on the water it is a large, rounded mountain, 1,000 or 1,200 feet high, of dignified pose and lofty style. It rises in very small terraces, and no soil can be discerned upon its ragged sides; yet scattered over them are small fir trees, their clinging roots penetrating the niches and crevices for sustenance. The water hereabouts is of unknown depth, and the steamer's course is within a few feet of the mighty wall of the mountain.

By this time our little steamer has carried us far within the great defile. We seem literally encompassed by the everlasting hills. They stand like the opposing hosts of armies forever petrified, on the verge of combat.

The configuration of these antagonistic mountain giants is markedly different.

As a rule, the great masses of the eastern range are nearer to us; with one or two notable exceptions are not so ravaged by cañons; have a lesser altitude, but are more redundant of form nearer to the lake. A feature of this side is the dome-like structure of many of the precipital walls rising from the water's edge. These overawing cliffs are not only in their entirety dome shaped, but their faces are themselves built up, or have weathered into, an infinitude of smaller domes. In many places the bluffs or the sharper slopes near them are finely fluted. These grooves are hundreds of feet long, and are formed by the cascades which in spring and early summer go bounding down them.

As the mountains run to the north the range rises to tremendous heights, the peculiar rounded forms still emphasized amidst the increased wildness and grandeur on every hand.

Black Cap, a massive, round, lordly rock, with a succession of domelets extending beneath it to the timber line near the shore, is a bald bluff boldly facing the lake, that will always attract attention.

Turn now to the western shore. Mark the difference between it and its rival. Of loftier height, greater variety of form, more exuberance of foliage, deeper penetration of gorge and cañon, it looms aloft, Cyclopean in its immensity.

With a boldness in conception audacious, the mighty flanks sweep toward the empyrean in curvilinear lines something to behold. If one falters, appalled at the daring that has carried it thus far, another takes up the task, and bears it upward. In all directions, at all angles, these mammoth spurs are carved out, the one object to be attained being to get as far heavenward as possible.

The ridges at the summit, thousands of feet above us, have been carved by Father Time into all manner of monumental forms. Sharp, incisive peaks, scenic effect! Who can depict their glory? Who can portray the fascination of the sight?

One of the most effective sights to show to man his utter insignificance, is to gaze upon the resistless power of water. This may be in many ways: the irresistible current of a river; the lashing of the tempest-tossed ocean; the overpowering deluge throwing itself over precipice or through rock-strewn gorge. Even so at the Dalles, "where the river is literally turned on edge, so narrow and profound being the chasm through which it flows that the huge proportions of its mighty flood are absolutely inverted"; not alone the terrible grandeur of the sight impresses itself on one, but the tremendous exhibition of power drives home the former, and clinches it there.

Perhaps the most delightful detour of several that can be made from Portland is by the Columbia River boats to Astoria, and thence to Ilwaco. At Ilwaco the Narrow Gauge Railway is taken·for Sealand, where connection is made by boat for South Bend, the chief town on Willapa Harbor. From South Bend the tourist takes boat for North Cove, where connection is made by stage, running along the ocean beach, to a point near Ocosta, on Gray's Harbor, at which point rail connection is made for Tacoma. If the passenger on arriving at South Bend, at which point there is an excellent hotel, does not care to prolong his trip, he can take the train on the Northern Pacific from there, reaching Tacoma via this branch line.

Portland, itself an old city, and the largest on the northwestern coast, wealthy and conservative, but by no means non-progressive, is an attractive place.

The Willamette Valley, the largest in Oregon, tumbles into the lap of Portland the products of its harvests, the fruitage from its vines and orchards, whence they are scattered over the world.

"From the summit of Robinson's Hill, a view that it is no extravagance to pronounce one of the finest in the world may be obtained. At one's feet lies the city, nestled in rich foliage. Stretching away for many miles may be seen the Columbia and Willamette rivers. But above all, bounded only by the limits of the horizon, is the great Cascade Range with all its glittering peaks. On the extreme right, seventy-eight miles distant as the·crow flies, is seen the snowy crown of Mount Jefferson; across the river, fifty-one miles distant, rises Mount Hood, one of the most beautiful mountains on the coast, and the pride and glory of Oregon; to the northeast stand out the crests of Mount Adams and Mount St. Helens, and in the same direction, but 100 miles away, may be descried the great Tacoma, the grandest mountain on the Pacific slope, and all five peaks radiant with eternal snow."

Tacoma, a beautiful city—a city of homes of taste and refinement—is a point from which one may radiate in many directions. The city itself is one of the most attractive to be found, and the wonder is that within such short time such a city has grown here.

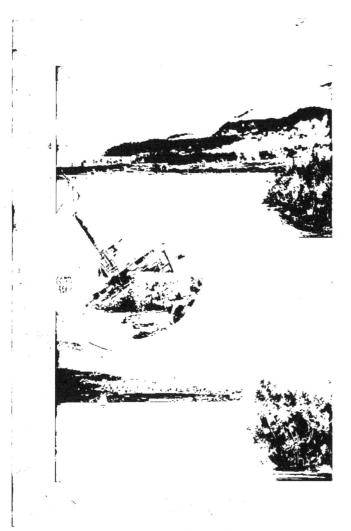

KOOTENAI LAKE.

LAKE CHELAN.

YELLOWSTONE PARK.

EARLY HISTORY—TRANSPORTATION FACILITIES— REGULATIONS, ETC.

HE Yellowstone Park! The gem of wonderland. The land of mystic splendor. Region of bubbling caldron and boiling pool with fretted rims, rivaling the coral in delicacy of texture and the rainbow in variety of color; of steaming funnels exhaling into the etherine atmosphere in calm, unruffled monotone and paroxysmal ejection vast clouds of fleecy vapor from the underground furnaces of the God of Nature. Sylvan parkland, where amidst the unsullied freshness of flower-strewn valley and bountiful woodland the native fauna of the land browse in fearless joy and wander wild and free, unfretted by sound of huntsman's horn, the long-drawn bay of the hound, and the sharp crack of the rifle.

Land of beauteous vale and laughing water, thundering cataract and winding ravine; realm of the Ice King and the Fire King; enchanted spot, where mountain and sea meet and kiss each other; where the murmurs of the river, as it meanders through heaven-blest valleys, become harsh and sullen amid the pine-covered hills which darken and throttle its joyous song, until, uncontrollable, it throws itself, a magnificent sheet of diamond spray and plunging torrent, over precipices, and rolls along an emerald flood betwixt cañon walls such as the eye of mortal hath seldom seen.

EARLY HISTORY.

JOHN COLTER — LANGFORD — WASHBURN — DE LACY — HAYDEN, ETC.— FIRST EXPLORATIONS.

Back early in the '6o's, and even before that time, vague stories were heard around the camp fires at the bivouacs of the trappers and mountaineers, of a wonderful locality unlike any other on earth, to be found upon the headwaters of the Yellowstone. By and by these tales floated in upon the little towns, hamlets, settlements, forts, etc., which constituted the western frontier.

As they flitted from camp to camp and from post to settlement, they lost nothing in the telling, and, coming from a class much given to exaggeration and romancing, they were set down largely as stories of a Munchausen type, and excited little credibility.

A few, however, upon investigation, became convinced that there was a solid basis of fact back of whatever embellishments many have surrounded these yarns, and determined to ascertain by actual exploration what it was.

So far as it is now possible to gather the evidence, John Colter was the first white man to proclaim to the world the existence of this region. This man's career must have been a thrilling one. He was a member of Lewis and Clark's expedition, and returned with a companion, when done with them, to the headwaters of the Jefferson Fork of the Missouri. Surprised by the Black-feet, his companion was killed, and he stripped naked and made to run the gauntlet. His singular escape is related in Irving's Astoria.

Another noted scout, plainsman, and mountaineer who told of the beauties of this country was the late James Bridger, but Bridger's reputation for picturesque embellishment of plain fact caused many to disbelieve much that he uttered.

It was not until 1870 and 1871 that the park country was first prominently brought to the attention of the world. Two men are, more than any others, deserving of the credit for making known the wonders of the Yellowstone Park. These men are Nathaniel P. Langford, an honored citizen of St. Paul, Minn., and the late Dr. Ferdinand V. Hayden, the well-known geologist and explorer.

Langford, an old mountaineer and resident of the far West, had long wanted to explore the headwaters of the Yellowstone. Finding a number of other Montana gentlemen of the same mind, he helped to organize, in 1870, an expedition which was known as the Washburn party, named after the surveyor general of Montana, who was made its chief.

In the May and June numbers of *Scribner's Monthly* — now the *Century Magazine* — for 1871, Langford described the adventures of this trip.

In 1871 Dr. Hayden, at that time the head of one of the United States Geological Surveys, with a large party of geologists, topographers, artists, and others, made the first extended and scientific survey of the region. Mr. Lang-ford also accompanied Dr. Hayden. The result of Hayden's explorations, coupled with his earnest recommendation that the country be reserved for all time to come for a national park, together with the drawings and photographs given to the public, evoked an interest which has steadily increased.

Dr. Hayden is dead. After a long life given to Western exploration and scientific research he rests from his labors. In the scientific world he will long be remembered for other work, as well as his labors here; but to the world at large, the Yellowstone Park will stand as his monument for all time to come, and a more lasting and more worthy one no man could wish.

Other men made explorations and reports — Col. Raynolds of the army,

MOUNT TACOMA.

THE OLYMPIAN, TACOMA, WASHINGTON. (Under Construction.)

in 1859–60; Capt. DeLacy in 1863, with a party of prospectors, and Lieut. Gustavus C. Doane in 1871, being the more important.

The latter officer had charge of the army escort which accompanied the Washburn-Langford expedition in 1870, and made a report to the Secretary of War which ranks as one of the best contributions to the literature anent the park.

TRANSPORTATION, REGULATIONS, POLICING, ETC.

From Livingston, Mont., the Northern Pacific has a branch road known as the Yellowstone Park branch line, extending to Cinnabar, at the northern edge of the park, a distance of fifty-one miles. At Cinnabar, the large and comfortable four and six horse stages of the Yellowstone Park Transportation Company are entered, and a tour of the park is made by the regular tourist by this method of transportation.

The park is intended as a great pleasure ground for the pleasure and instruction of the people. It is under the direct control of the United States Government, and a sufficient number of soldiery are kept there the year through to patrol the park and afford a watchful supervision of it, prevent acts of vandalism, enforce the regulations governing the use of the park, and see that all parties have the protection of the laws of the land.

It is an offense punished by summary ejection to tamper with any of the objects in the park, kill or capture game, be careless in the use of camp fires, etc. Fishing with hook and line is allowable.

Under Government supervision new roads are being opened, and old ones are constantly kept repaired.

The transportation facilities through the park deserve special mention.

The horses used are not the wild, unreliable bronco of the plains and mountains, but good, steady stage horses. Harness and coaches are of the world-renowned Concord pattern, which means that strength, safety, and durability are the prime objects aimed at. The coaches are made specially for tourist travel, and so as to allow the occupant the freest outlook possible. The best drivers to be obtained are used, and are under orders to afford all possible facilities and information to passengers to see, and understand what they see.

The tour of the park at any time during the regular season is a source of pleasure. The writer made it during the last week of August. If, however, one can choose the time, and desires to see it when the hills and valleys and parks are clothed in their freshest green, when the streams are fullest, when the mountain flowers are crowding bud and leaf to their fruition, dressing out the slopes and vales in summer attire, and emitting upon a balmy air odors of delicious fragrance, the early part of the season is to be preferred. June seems to meet all these conditions the best, and those botanically inclined will probably obtain their greatest pleasure at that time.

A word as to the fauna.

The domains of the park are a haven of refuge to all animals for thousands of square miles about. They know this, and frequent the park in large numbers. Bear, deer, elk, antelope, buffalo, mountain sheep, and all the other varieties of wild animals are here, and are very often seen as the stages roll along, or from the hotels. They are very tame, and molest no one. Indeed, the bears are scavengers for the hotels, and the guests flock out at night to see Bruin gorge himself and go rolling away when filled.

There are large herds of deer and elk, and probably 300 buffalo roaming o'er the valleys and hills. The habitat of the latter in summer is usually in the region about Yellowstone Lake.

The fishing to be found here can not be surpassed. Nearly all the waters of the park contain fish of some sort. Mountain trout are everywhere, grayling are found in the Madison and Gallatin rivers, and whitefish in the Yellowstone, Madison, and Gardiner.

The angler, however, will probably find his greatest sport at Yancey's. Here in the Yellowstone, after it has plunged through the Grand Cañon, is afforded a chance for the fisherman seldom, if ever, equaled.

LIVINGSTON TO CINNABAR—CINNABAR TO MAMMOTH HOT SPRINGS—
MAMMOTH HOT SPRINGS.

The ride from Livingston to Cinnabar will interest many. The Yellowstone River bank is followed by the railroad, and many fine glimpses of the lovely river afforded. The valley itself, several miles wide as a rule, is the remnant of an ancient lake bed whose floor is strewn with glaciated bowlders, affording views of rocky, rugged cuts and spurs, and again showing fine stretches of valley and upland plain to gaze upon. There are two cañons through which the river and railroad run, which, were it not for the greater cañon to be seen in the park itself, would attract attention. As it is, they suffer greatly by comparison. Throughout the entire ride to Cinnabar the mountains on both sides are stately, and increase in height and massiveness as the train speeds southward. Cinnabar Mountain is worthy of attention. It is a group of vertical beds, at one point nearly two thousand feet high. Extending from summit to base is a reddish band of arenaceous clay seventy-five feet wide, formerly supposed to be cinnabar, which gave name to the mountain. The Devil's Slide is found here. It is formed by two walls of rock, parallel, and protruding from the mountain, making it a very striking object.

From Cinnabar the ride to Mammoth Hot Springs is over an excellent road. I wish here to emphasize the superiority of Yellowstone Park roads. To me, one of the pleasantest features of the park tour is the roads, with their lovely vistas, graceful curves, strong bridges, and usually good road-bed.

Gardiner River, along which the road winds from Cinnabar, has its source at the southern base of Electric Peak, flows south to work around Bunsen Peak, and then turns to the north and flows into the Yellowstone at Cinnabar. After a ride of eight miles to the south the road, after a long climb, turns abruptly to the east. First the Mammoth Hot Springs Hotel is seen, and the instant after there breaks upon the eye one of the strangest, most fascinating sights to be seen on this planet; something utterly unlike anything elsewhere. It is the gorgeously arrayed — for gorgeous they are — terraces or cliffs of the Mammoth Hot Springs.

Mammoth Hot Springs.

If the effect upon others is the same that it was upon me, the first impressions of these strange phenomena, upon examination, will be disappointing. Their great beauty and wonderful peculiarities are not revealed to the mind in their fullness at one fell swoop. It requires time, thought, reflection, and the workings of imagination to some extent, to grasp the tremendous meaning of all this, to assimilate it mentally. If the tourist who makes the regularly scheduled trip of the park will, after his return to this point, clamber around and over these terraces of living waters and cliffs of dead and ancient matter, he will find, upon the second visit, that the impression left is far greater and far more satisfactory than was the first, especially if he be careful to add to his repertoire some things not before seen.

Dr. Hayden when he first viewed these springs named them the "White Mountain Hot Spring," from the snowy whiteness of the large expanse of terraces seen from some points. He compared them to "frozen cascades," a not inapt illustration.

In some places the intense whiteness of the mass is absolutely dazzling. Again it resembles huge walls of congealed pitch. At another place the most delicate combinations of colors are shown — pink, lemon, orange, cream, artistically intermingled.

The guide-books, easily obtained, will give in detail the objects of greatest interest. Among these are the Liberty Cap, an ancient geyser mummy, Devil's Thumb, the Jupiter, Minerva, and Pulpit terraces, the Elephant's Back, Cupid's Cave, Devil's Kitchen, Orange Geyser, etc.

There are two points that many fail to see. These are located far back up the terraced cliffs — easy of access, however — and are marked by sign-posts as the Stalactic and Stygian caves. In the former — both caves are small — are stalactites and stalagmites very pretty to see. The latter, or the Cave of Death, is so impregnated with arsenic as to be dangerous to life, and around the entrance are the remains of birds, bugs, etc., that have died from inhaling the poisonous fumes. The writer picked up the body of a little yellow and green bird that had evidently but just died from the effects of these arsenical vapors.

From a point called Admiration Point, and very justly named, the sightseer has a view of the springs and pools, just below him, that fairly takes his breath. This point is just above Cupid's Cave. Time and space prevent an attempt at description, but it is one of the most beautiful sights to be found on earth. The deep, resplendent pools, or lakelets, of deepest emerald in the center, at other parts of gorgeous colors startling in effect, and boiling in pulsating jets, cause the observer to stand speechless.

In wandering among the springs there will be noticed in some places large, white, fan-like growths of a jelly-like nature, similar in appearance to the ffoating leaves of pond lilies, or of a membranous character. In other places these forms are of a filamentary nature, of a texture most delicate, and if in a spring having a current, are possessed of a flowing motion, graceful in the extreme. In appearance they show a sheen like finest satin.

These forms are of a vegetable nature, being microscopic algæ, more or less coated and incrusted with travertine — a form of limestone deposited from hot springs — of which the terraces are built up. In the bowls of hot water where the temperature exceeds 150° Fahrenheit, the algous growth is white; in the cooler water, depending upon the temperature, it is of a green, orange, red, yellow, etc.

A full discussion of this interesting subject, and, too, more or less intelligible to the average reader, is found in the report for 1887–88 of the United States Geological Survey. It is contributed by Mr. W. H. Weed of the survey, who has specially investigated the subject.

MAMMOTH HOT SPRINGS TO LOWER GEYSER BASIN — GOLDEN GATE —
    BUNSEN PEAK — SWAN LAKE VALLEY — OBSIDIAN CLIFF — NORRIS
    GEYSER BASIN — GIBBON RIVER, FALLS, AND CAÑON.

It requires just one week to make the tour of the park and return, from Livingston. There are many interesting things en route.

Bunsen Peak is a noble mountain seen directly south from the Hot Springs Hotel. Between this and Terrace Mountain the road winds through Golden Gate Cañon.

From the time of leaving the hotel we are climbing until Swan Lake Valley is reached, 1,000 feet above the hotel plateau.

Just before reaching Golden Gate, which is a very striking object, where one mile of road cost $14,000, a region of protruding white and gray rocks is passed. At all angles, in all shapes, sizes, and positions, they form a quaint scene, and remind one of Rip Van Winklian days, and we almost look to see Hendrick Hudson and his dumb companions appear in fantastic attire rolling about the mountain's flanks.

The road through Golden Gate is a winding curiosity. At the western end

SHOSHONE LAKE.

MINERVA TERRACE; HOTEL AND VALLEY.

MAMMOTH HOT SPRINGS.

HOTEL MAMMOTH HOT SPRINGS

WEST FROM GOLDEN GATE.

GOLDEN GATE.

of the cañon Swan Valley and Lake spread out before us a lovely pastoral scene, with lofty mountain peaks looking down upon it.

Following Swan Lake Valley comes Willow Creek Park. This is a most lovely and interesting spot. The whole valley here rather contracted, is covered by a dense growth of low, symmetric willow bushes, in the midst of which Obsidian Creek meanders.

Beaver Lake and Obsidian Cliff, especially the latter, are among the interesting points in this part of the park.

The cliff is one-half mile long and from 150 to 200 feet high. The southern end is formed of volcanic glass or obsidian, as true a glass as any artificially produced. The roadway at its base is constructed across the talus, and is emphatically a glass road. Huge fragments of the obsidian, black and shining, some of it streaked with white seams, line the road. Small pieces are also plentiful. This flow of glass came from a high plateau to the east-northeast. Numerous vent pits or apparent craters have been discovered on this plateau. Mr. J. P. Iddings, of the United States Geological Survey, who has made a special study of Obsidian Cliff, contributes to the survey report for 1885-86, a paper that has in it much that is of interest to the unscientific mind.

As Norris Geyser Basin is neared, the hot spring and geyser-like character of the country is manifest. These vast areas of sinter are very unattractive in general appearance, the interest centering wholly in the wonderful phenomena displayed therein.

The outlook over Norris Geyser Basin is a strange and weird one. Columns of steam wafted skyward, groanings and rumblings heard beneath us, violent and intermittent eruptions of hot water and steam, all over an extended area desolate in the extreme, form a strange medley of sight and sound, the interesting and uninteresting. Some beautiful springs and pools and quaint mud pots are found here near the road. From the basin the road crosses a geyserite plain, white and naked.

Ascending the little wooded divide, the Gibbon Meadows or Elk Park burst upon the vision, followed by the rugged Gibbon Cañon. The contrast between the Norris Basin just left and this region is refreshing in the extreme.

Beryl Spring is a beautiful pool. The circular, boiling spring, some fifteen feet in diameter and near the roadside, with its deep, beryl hue, and steam clouds, is beautiful beyond power of pen to describe.

Gibbon Falls, somewhat over eighty feet high, a rather fan-shaped fall, is in the midst of a cañon scene of rugged grandeur.

Throughout this portion of the park the road is a fine one, furnishing at every turn captivating views.

From Gibbon Cañon the road ascends and winds through a park region. The myriad sylvan, rustic, and woodland scenes presented all through the great park as the stages bowl along, justify the appellation of park, given to the reservation, equally as well as do the great springs, geysers, and cañon. Indeed, this title could hardly be appropriately bestowed on the strength of the latter alone.

From the plateau between Gibbon Cañon and the charming Firehole River and basin, into which the road soon descends, one of the most extensive and refreshing landscapes of the entire trip is beheld. Low, rolling mountains, overcast with black forests, rise to the horizon, while between are sweeping valleys with sinuous rivers and gloomy, ragged ravines.

After the long day's ride it is a pleasure to find rest at the large, roomy hotel located at Lower Geyser Basin.

The general appearance of the Lower Geyser Basin is far more pleasing than is that at the Norris.

In the cooler evening the sight from the hotel over the wide expanse of plain and mountain is one of peace, content, serenity, unless, perchance, a geyser break the quiet monotony. The low hills and mountains far away, dark and slumberous, form a splendid background for the countless pillars and clouds of steam ascending from all directions.

I had the fortune to witness the Fountain Geyser in play. It was late in the evening. I had scrambled around its wide double basin with beaded fringes and wonderful water, leaned out as far as I dared to gaze down into its rounded geyser tube, and admired it in its great beauty and splendor. At last, when I had given it up and just turned hotelward, it suddenly sprang into action, and the ebullition was one to challenge comparison with any in the park. Enormous quantities of water were ejected in a frothing, boiling, seething mass of more than snow-white, foamy crystals. It bobs up and down somewhat, and spurts of foam rise to heights of fifteen to thirty feet. The general effect is that of a magnificent fountain, its compact wall of water, oblong and irregular in appearance, with lovely spray balls shooting out from the edges, all brilliant and glittering in the expiring light of day.

To the east of the fountain are, in some respects, the most interesting paint pots in the park. Some 40 x 60 feet across, its color in a general way being that of dull or grayish-light terra cotta, it resembles an enormous basin of boiling, clayey mush. It is a great curiosity, and should not be missed by the tourist.

EXCELSIOR GEYSER AND UPPER GEYSER BASIN.

It is ten miles between the two Geyser basins. The drive is an intensely interesting one. Winding through the enchanting valley of the Firehole River, through grassy mead and piney arcades, the greatest geyser in the world, and the most entrancing spot of this wonderland to many, is soon reached.

Excelsior Geyser is very independent, and it is only at long and irregular intervals that it reaches a state of fermentation. When that time does come, it is worth a journey across the continent to see it. As the glory of the sun immeasurably transcends that of the moon and stars, so are the beauties and the stupendous exhibitions of this geyser beyond compare with the others of the geyser family.

Long considered as a mammoth spring — excelling in size and loveliness all other springs — its true character did not for many years show itself. It will remain quiescent for years, and then break forth in ebullitions of indescribable grandeur, throwing out such quantities of thermal water that the Firehole River at its base goes tearing through the valley at flood-tide, a torrent of burning, scalding water. It also vomits forth large rocks, hurling them high in the air and scattering them over the adjacent plain.

The geyser and Prismatic Lake, or spring, near by, are across the river from the road, and are reached by a foot-bridge.

Heavy clouds of steam are continually rising from the place and obscure the vision, but in the rifts one may get glimpses of the pristine loveliness of the pools. The entire surroundings are weird in the extreme, and call to mind the witch scene in " Macbeth." As we endeavor to penetrate with the eye to the center of the Excelsior, we would not be surprised to see the three witches faintly outlined there.

If ever there was a place where the powers of the subterranean world have a chance to give full play to their effervescence, and show forth their powers of gymnasticism, it is in the Upper Basin. To some the idea of orchestration will present itself. An odd orchestra this. Each member of it plays away in his own peculiar manner, utterly oblivious of the rest. If perchance any number of them get to work together, 'tis confusion worse confounded to the audience round about.

The peculiar features of this place are well known. Old Faithful, the Giant and Giantess, Lion and Lioness, the Castle, Oblong, Splendid, Bee Hive, Grotto, etc., are almost household words.

This basin is differentiated from the others, in that it contains the largest number of highly active geysers in the park. Nearly every prominent geyser gives more or less violent and grand displays, shooting forth its contents at certain intervals high into the air, in various and fanciful forms.

THE RIDE TO YELLOWSTONE LAKE — INSPIRING SCENERY — MAGNIFI-
CENT FORESTS — KEPPLER'S CASCADES — THE LAKE.

One of the most enjoyable experiences to the writer, in the entire round of pleasure, was the ride from the Geyser Basins to Yellowstone Lake.

The road is new, laid out in graceful curves, and for much of the distance is as well graded and kept as in any city park; indeed, it strongly reminds of one at many points. Long, curving stretches of road through shady and refreshing woodland are succeeded by little parks and clearings. It winds first through the lovely valley of the Upper Firehole, then twists and crawls through the wild and narrow cañon of Spring Creek. At places in this little cañon the rocks stand out in jutting crags threatening and wild. The road gradually ascends through narrow defiles, around abrupt mountain sides, heading tangled ravines, until the summit of the Continental Divide is reached. The latter part of the drive to the lake is through a luxuriant park country teeming with delicious bits of scenery. Along this arboreous way there are three spots worthy of mention.

About two miles from the Upper Basin the road passes close by Keppler's Cañon and Cascades. These are easily seen, and are worthy of a visit while the stages stop.

At Shoshone Point, where Shoshone Lake is visible, the view is one never to be forgotten. Far away in the distance a glimpse of the sleeping lake is had, deep down among the mountains mantled with the luxuriant foliage which covers the face of nature everywhere hereabout. The road winds about a projecting point, above which the shaggy forest towers, while below lurks a ravine black and rugged also with trees. Trees everywhere, as if rejoicing that there is one spot of God's footstool where they can grow and expand untouched by ax and unscathed, let us hope, by fire.

From the tongue of mountain shot forth, and around which the road runs, the prospect is an extended one. Between the lake — and near it — and the vast army of trees beneath us is a bit of light green, a little park, an oasis 'midst the somber silence which broods over all. Mountains rise on every hand. As the stage drives on, we feel that we have been blessed with an inspired picture. When near the west arm — the thumb of the wonderful lake we are soon to see — the road winds high above a region of parks, and dells, and little lakes, and arborean retreats simply entrancing in their loveliness. Such bits of landscape are like old wine, rich and rare. In the midst of such a scene the Yellowstone Lake breaks on the sight. It is a picture for an artist. I think no one can really form an idea, from description alone, of the great beauty of this mountain sea. Simply as a large and lovely lake it is of surpassing grace. Island jewels rise from its limpid depths. Its shores, at the water's edge low hills and pine-clad, rise as they retreat, and finally sweep up into some of the noblest, most commanding of peaks, with coronets of mountain firs and pines swept by the mighty winds of heaven and baptized by the snow-clouds wafted in from the mists of the sea.

On the lake shore, where the lunch station is situated, are found some of the prettiest hot springs in the park. Here also are seen some most attractive paint pots. These are really the best of their kind to be found in the park, and the sightseer can stand for hours and continually see new wonders in these large, boiling caldrons of clay, marvelous both in texture and color. Here, too, one can catch his fish in the lake, flop him over into the boiling spring kettle and cook him, and then eat him, all without moving from one spot.

At the north end of the lake, near the point where the Yellowstone River leaves it, is the Yellowstone Lake Hotel. It occupies a commanding position in the center of a clearing among the trees, with the side toward the lake open. The hotel faces the lake, and the view afforded across its waters of the finest mountain scenery of the park would please an enthusiast. It is a scene of rare beauty.

The hotel is large, new, cheerful; and with its delightful surroundings is probably the resting spot which will be most often thought of by travelers after the incidents of the trip have become a thing of the past and are lived again in imagination only.

YELLOWSTONE LAKE TO THE GRAND CAÑON — THE RIVER — MUD GEYSER — THE GRAND CAÑON.

From the lake to the cañon the fine scenery continues. It seems as if this portion of the park intended to make up for lack of geysers, etc., by a general landscape far finer and more beautiful, and it does it. For most of the distance the road hugs the Yellowstone River, here fresh from the lake. Many delightful river views are vouchsafed us.

Mud Geyser, or Mud Volcano, is a phenomenon. A deep, vertical pit in the side of the mountain — conical in shape, lead-colored, and having an opening or cave leading back into the hill — with great industry continually ejects a mushy, thick mass of clay, with much belching of steam. In its violent throes it seems to be uselessly endeavoring to purge itself of an overloaded stomach.

Hayden Valley is a phantasy. No one who has a love for "the good, the true, the beautiful," can look out upon this glowing exhibition of waving plain and not feel the spirit within stirred to something better for it. It can not be described; to do justice to it, it must be seen.

Some time before the Grand Cañon and upper falls are reached, the indications are strong that a change is at hand. The river goes skurrying along in a greater hurry, as if it had an important engagement which it was in great danger of missing. Soon its hurried gait changes to one of still greater speed, and it foams and dashes along in utter abandon. Now a dull, muffled roar is heard, and through the thick veil of pines which curtains the river we catch instantaneous views of it, pounding and racing along in flashes of yeasty foam, until it pours over the first falls a dazzling mass of mist and frothing torrent.

The road, now within an area fairly overflowing with grandeur, soon affords us our first look at the great cañon. It is for an instant only, but it gives us a foretaste of the pleasures in store for us in the near future.

After a generous lunch at the commodious and excellent hotel at the cañon, arrangements were made to spend the afternoon in rambling about the cañon walls. A companion and myself provided ourselves with horses, and sallied forth.

For two reasons my visit to the Yellowstone Cañon was the particular feature, the *sine qua non*, of the trip.

For years I had climbed, and ridden, and camped among the stupendous gorges of the Green and Colorado rivers, in the land of cañons. I had become fascinated with *fine* cañon scenery, and desired to view for its own sake this, to me, new thing in cañons.

Again, I wished to compare it with those with which I was familiar, especially in the light of eulogy which has been showered upon it.

I shall institute no comparisons between these types of cañon structure. None can well be made. In their general characteristics, structural peculiarities, colors, etc., there is such marked dissimilarity that a comparison between them would be about as senseless and ridiculous as to compare a blooded Percheron or Clydesdale horse with a thoroughbred trotting horse. Both are cañons, as both are horses, but each is *sui generis*. Both are fine, deserve what has been said of them, and are in no true sense rivals.

Riding away we reached the brink of the cañon at a commanding point, midway, perhaps, between Lookout Point of the guide-books and Inspiration Point. As we rode out to where a view of the great trench opened before us, I dismounted, walked out on to a projecting ledge and looked forth with the greatest curiosity.

At last I stood upon the edge of the great chasm; saw the wondrously sculptured forms which bristled upon each league of wall; the river throwing itself over the narrow precipice and rolling far below, a beautiful, winding ribbon of green. I saw before me the inspiration of artists, the theme of orators and lecturers; the subject which has produced an unbounded amount of fervid word-painting; which has been sung by the good, the bad, the indifferent in the realm of letters and poesy.

When one has heard and read so much of anything as of the Grand Cañon of the Yellowstone, if ever the time comes when the actual scene itself stands before one, and the former child of the imagination must step forth and give place to the real, the result is very apt to be a disappointment.

It is not so here. The great gorge is a study, a revelation, a wonder, and deserving of many and strong adjectives, and will stand much exuberance of language and strong figurative treatment in the telling of its story.

It is by all odds, to the writer, the greatest jewel of the many found here, and in its great magnificence and grandeur eclipses geysers, hot springs, paint pots, lakes, and rivers. Indeed, it may be almost said to be a compendium of all else here, save the lake itself. After a few moments spent at the place noted, we cantered ahead to Inspiration Point, the farthest point visited usually by the tourist.

From this promontory, thrown well out from the general western wall, there is afforded a tremendous sweep of vision both up and down the cañon.

No man can begin to describe the variety of effect experienced, nor the wealth of detail in color, form, depth, etc., seen from any one of the many points of view presented, unless he can sit there for hours, climb up and down the walls, study, absorb, and make a part of himse'f what he sees.

The prodigality of detail in every respect is enormous.

The friable walls, scraped and chiseled and cracked and washed by rain, ice, snow, frost, are fairly crowded with pinnacles, spires, grottoes, and precipitous cliff points. Very like old castellated ruins are many of the cliffs seen along the face and crest of the cañon walls.

What adds to the weird grandeur of the place, are the numbers of eagles' nests perched on the sharp tips of many of the buttresses and towers, round which in wide circling flight, the very ideal of aerial motion, some parent bird sweeps. Suddenly swooping to the river, cutting the air with the rapidity almost of the lightning's flash, it rises from the water bearing aloft to its hungry eaglets an unlucky fish. The plaintive cries of the birds floating up from the hollow space below are strangely mournful.

From Inspiration Point, one of the most affecting sights is the far-distant view of the lower falls. Scarcely larger than a hand do they seem, a white, silvery sheen set in the center of a black girth of tree-clad cliffs and mountains. Too far away to hear the sound thereof, the sight alone is real. To hear them the imagination must be called in play.

The best view of the great or lower falls is obtained from Lookout Point. There seem to be two points of this name, one about two miles from the falls, the other so-named on the maps of the United States Geological Survey, the official survey of the Government, and distant some eight or ten miles. The one herein referred to is that nearest the falls. Its elevation above the water is about 1,000 feet. The cañon walls are in no place more than 1,200 feet high.

The outlook from this point is certainly one of striking power and beauty. The distance is enough to render the perspective the most perfect, the falls being near enough to stand out in sufficient detail, and yet far enough away to prevent a contracted, dwarfed aspect, and to invest them with a stately, quiet dignity which seems peculiarly appropriate to them.

I left the warm bed at the hotel at "5 o'clock in the morning," muffled myself in heavy overcoat, and by 6 o'clock sat alone on the vertical cliff here, and feasted my eyes and soul. It was damp and cold; the sun was trying hard to shine through the heavy masses of cloud and vapor which hung over the cañon, dampening the foliage at the crest of either wall. Down below in the vast abyss itself it was dank and gray; the glowing colors, so resplendent at noonday, were smothered and subdued, in truth, were deep in cañon slumber; quiet reigned, save for the low, distant, deadened rumble of the fall, which "loud from its rocky caverns" was wafted up on the fluctuating sound waves

6

from the depths; save for the melancholy cries of a forlorn eagle soaring through the cañon gloom.

The communion with Nature at such a place and at such an hour is an experience in one's career. The falls can be seen then — when they can be seen — as they can at no other hour. Hovering over them, enveloping them, hiding them, now in total, now in partial eclipse, floats a sheet, a cloud, a robe, of billowy mist. Long I sit and watch the struggle as the old day god tries to penetrate this spectral veil and scatter it to the tree-tops crowning the heights. Cold and hungry I at last turn from the inspired spot and retrace my steps, following all the windings of the cliff to where the trail turns away to the hotel on the hill.

I can still see that morning vision,—can see the caps and spires flashing in the sporadic gleams of the slow-conquering sun,—can hear the eagle's cry, the muffled roar of the cataract,—see the mist roll in splendor away, the dull sleeping walls. Far away, it yet moves and breathes and lives.

It is probably true that to the majority of spectators the greater fall excites more interest than the upper or lesser fall. I confess that to me the upper fall was the greater attraction. There is beyond question a superb spectacle, superiority of power, the effect of crushing, irresistible force, and withal, a stately, noble dignity in the lower fall that compels the homage of the beholder.

But there is in the upper fall a life, action, vivacity, energy that are simply irresistible. In a great rollicking, bellowing mass of snow-crested foam, dashing and threshing, dancing and prancing, jumping and thumping, crashing and flashing, in one wild paroxysm of mountain glee, it leaps over the ledge into the pool below. From the seething mass at the bottom of the fall the spray clouds chase each other around the walled glen. From the fall itself the tiny crystal spray-drops leap and flash and shimmer and sparkle in the sunlight, overflowing with humor and mirth. Rampant with animation and joy, it represents the tireless activity and energy of youth, while the greater cataract typifies the more mature and sedate manhood.

Grand and glorious pageant; vision mighty and eternal; for unnumbered æons thou hast been slowly, through the attritive powers given thee by Nature's God, working out thy destiny. With a perseverance sublime, by the power of torrent and beat of wave, the rush of the avalanche, the grinding of the glacier, the hot breath of the geyser, the subtle uplifting of the frost, the downpouring from the clouds; by all the powers of earth and sky, the wind and hail, the lightning's glare, the thunder's crash, hast thou worked onward, channeling the mountains, sculpturing the hills, painting the cliffs, that man, the noblest of God's creations, might stand before thee in awe and rapture, and feel himself uplifted to that spirit land from whence he came.

GEYSER BASIN.

GIANT GEYSER.

OLD FAITHFUL.

GIANT GEYSER.

UPPER GEYSER BASIN.

YELLOWSTONE LAKE.

THE TRAGEDY OF THE LITTLE BIG HORN,

OR, CUSTER'S LAST STRUGGLE.

I AM seated on an historic spot. All about me are the evidences of an awful tragedy. Not now of the blood-curdling sort, where ghastly corpses, dead animals, and all the accompanying features of fearful carnage lie about me, for time has thoroughly obliterated all these traces of the fearful event.

I am in a city of the dead; of those who died far from home and friends — aye! far from civilization itself — in a mad, fruitless struggle to save themselves from the most horrible of deaths. But, successful as they had been heretofore, they were caught in Death's trap at last; their fate had overtaken them, and these little white, silent headstones, scattered in groups all around me, attest the sad end of a fight they had thought fraught with brilliant possibilities.

The scene before me is a peaceful one.

Round about me lies an upland country, washed and carved into a billowy sea of hills, coulées, and ridges. Back of me, many miles distant, are the rocky hills and bleak, scarped cliffs, all cut and scarred by ravines and gullies, from whence issued forth those who now are sleeping around me.

Below me, stretching far away in the subdued light of a sinking western sun, is a wide valley, "fair as the garden of the Lord." Winding through it in silvery and graceful curves is a river, its sinuous course plainly marked by a splendid growth of cottonwoods.

Over to my left rises a bold and somewhat irregular line of clay bluffs, following up and forming the right bank of the river. Still back of these bluffs, and also of the knoll upon which I am seated, is a rolling plateau extending in alternating divide and depression back to the high, bluffy hills before noted.

Dotting the slopes immediately around me, here and there in thick bunches, now in scattering threes and fours, and farther away singly and in twos, are the little white marble slabs.

Now all is still, save as the wind rustles the grass and sings a plaintive requiem about the white monuments.

All day I have been riding over this scene of bloodshed and defeat, Custer's last battle ground, and now, after my hard day's ride, I sit down on the spot where Custer himself fell, near the battle monument, and try to imagine the feelings of that fated band as they fought against time, hoping and praying that help might yet come. But the sun of their destiny was set, and as the monarch of the day slowly sank behind the western hills, his last rays were cast upon a field strewn with the still and blanching bodies of Long Hair and his hitherto invincible troopers. Here was their Waterloo.

> Last noon beheld them full of lusty life,
> Last eve in beauty's circle proudly gay.
> The midnight brought the signal sound of strife;
> The morn, the marshaling of arms; the day,
> Battle's magnificently stern array!
> The thunder clouds close o'er it, which, when rent,
> The earth is covered thick with other clay,
> Which her own clay shall cover, heaped and pent,
> Rider and horse — friend, foe — in one red burial blent.

RIDING OVER THE BATTLE-GROUND — ITS APPEARANCE SIXTEEN
YEARS AFTER.

In the "wee sma' hours" of the morning a light touch from the porter aroused me from slumber, and rising from my berth, whereon I had thrown myself in the early evening divested only of my coat, I prepared to exchange the comforts of a Pullman for I knew not what. When the train stopped I found myself at some distance from the station-building at Custer, Mont.

Ever since the disastrous battle of the Little Big Horn I had felt a strong desire to visit that battle-field. Deeply interested as I had ever been in the battles of the War of the Rebellion, yet somehow I felt a greater longing to visit this far-away, isolated spot, so full of the tragic, the pathetic, the sad-dening. I am glad that I did. The trip is easily made, and a visit to the spot where Custer and his brave fellows struggled against such fearful odds is well worth the time required to make it. This fight and the campaign of 1876 by Generals Crook, Terry and Miles was, with one exception, the last Indian fight of any magnitude. Ute, Apache, Nez Percé, Modoc, Navajo, all save the Sioux and their allies, seemed to have been whipped into a wholesome respect for the power of the Government. This campaign taught the Sioux a lesson which has lasted, and they are now content to remain on their reserva-tions far from the towns and railroads of the West, now being rapidly populated.

After breakfast, taking my seat beside the stage driver, we started. Our course was to the southward, up the valley of Big Horn River itself.

About thirty miles south from Custer station Fort Custer, a large and well-appointed post, is located, high up on the bluffs in the angle formed by the junction of the two Horn rivers.

All day, until 4 P. M., we rolled up these glorious valleys of the great Crow Indian Reservation.

Upon the morning following my arrival at the Crow agency I mounted a good horse, and in company with my guide started upon my tour of the battle-ground.

The river banks and bottom are fringed with luxuriant foliage, and amidst this, on both sides of the river, and taking up much territory, were the tepees of the Cheyennes on that fatal 25th of June.

Following them, tracing the course up the stream, were the Brulé Sioux, the Ogalallas, Minncoujoux, Sans Ares, Uncapapas, and a few Blackfeet. There were also some renegade Arrapahoes, Santees, and Nez Percés. The bulk of this Indian village, encampment, city, or whatever one wishes to call it, extended for four miles or more up stream, with scattering tepees spreading to the south for another mile. At the point where the Indians were located the bottom varies from one to two miles in width.

A large part of this particular portion of the river bottom is now fenced in for Indian farms, grain fields, etc. At the time of the battle no such obstructions, of course, were there.

The western line of the valley is a wide plateau or plain, rising 100 to 200 feet and more above it, with gradual slopes, and penetrated by numerous creeks and ravines.

The eastern side is for the most part composed of dun-colored clay hills, 200 to 400 feet high, usually very abrupt, in many places absolutely vertical, and carved out by erosion into all manner of rounded symmetric forms, with ravines and hog-backs running back from the river. At the summit many little knolls and projections are seen overlooking the valley.

After a long ride the guide diverged to the west, and riding to a spot behind which was a little draw or coulée, thick with young trees, announced to me that we were on the ground where the meerschaum-colored tepee of Ta-Tonka-e-Yotanka, "the bull that sits down," formerly stood.

From thence we rode eastward to Ash Point, or Ash Hollow, so named from ash trees growing there, the point where Reno formed his skirmish line and where he sheltered himself in the timber.

At that time the bottom was very thickly timbered. Some of the trees have been burned and cut down since then. Near this point also stood the tepee of Gaul, and here his wife and young boy were killed by Reno's command.

Just back of this place a few hundred feet, now in the edge of an immense wire-fenced field, is the first striking memento of that fated day.

A small white headstone of marble, standing about two feet above the ground, bore the inscription:

DONALD · McINTOSH.

LIEUT. CO. G.

7TH U. S. CAV.,

FELL HERE

JUNE 25, 1876.

This typifies the inscriptions on all officers' headstones. The soldiers' markers were simply:

U. S. SOLDIER

7TH CAVALRY

FELL HERE

JUNE 25, 1876.

Surrounded by the long and dying grass, McIntosh's tombstone stood alone, far from any of its fellows, a silent, eloquent, forcible reminder of a day long gone by, when hell in its fury seemed to have broken loose here.

One other little memorial of that red day, as touching in its location and exile as that of McIntosh, is also visible from near this spot. Away over on the ashen-hued bluffs across the river to the east, almost at the top of the long steep hill, is another tiny, white dot. When Reno left the timber here, Dr. DeWolf was one of those who, in trying to escape, became separated from the main body. He got across the river, his horse was killed near the bluffs, and he started to scale them on foot. The Indians, already on the bluffs, lay in wait for and shot him when he had almost reached the top. The little marble stone marks the spot where he fell.

From Ash Point we rode to where Reno, in his panic-stricken retreat, recrossed the Little Horn.

A rather lengthy ride then found us at Reno's Crossing of the river, the ford where he crossed to make his attack. Fording the stream, we dismounted among the young timber and bushes lining the stream, and ate lunch. Before lunch was finished two Indian girls came down to the river. The younger, tall, slender, and graceful, dressed in bright, clean scarlet, was a picture. With her jet-black hair hanging in shining plaits, her piercing eyes and handsome face, she was the most comely, sylph-like Indian maiden I have ever seen.

Mounting our horses, lunch over, we cantered back, on the trail that Custer and Reno followed, for a ride of several miles to Lookout Hill, or Point, which we ascended. This was the point where Custer and his officers obtained their first view of the valley of the Greasy Grass, as the Sioux call the Little Horn.

YELLOWSTONE FALLS.

GRAND CANON OF THE YELLOWSTONE.

After a survey of the region, spurring our horses forward, we in time found ourselves climbing the gentle acclivities which led up to Reno's old rifle-pits, now almost obliterated.

The most noticeable feature of the spot is the number of blanched skulls and bones of horses which lie scattered about. A short distance from the pits — which are rather rounded, and follow the outline of the hills in shape — and in a slight hollow below them, are more bones of horses. This is where the wounded were taken, and the hospital established, and the horses kept.

Our course now lay over the hills and knolls, and the pretty little coulées between, to where Custer fought his last battle. It was from three to three and a half miles distant to the north, and out of sight from where the rifle-pits were.

From the wavy summit line of the bluffs the ground slopes in an irregular broken way back to the northeast and east, into a coulée that forms the passage to the ford *which Custer aimed for and never reached*.

The ground about the battle-field is now a national cemetery. It is inclosed by a wire fence, and there are several hundred acres of it. It might be cared for in a manner somewhat better than it is. During one of my visits there a Crow Indian rode up to the gate and deliberately turned his herd of horses into the inclosure to graze.

As I rode into the grounds, after fording and recrossing the river where Custer failed, the first object to greet my sight was a small inclosure with large mound and headstone, which marked the spot where Lieut. Crittenden fell. At one corner, and outside of it, stood the regulation marble slab which marks the place where each body on the field was found. This one stated that there Lieut. Calhoun was killed.

At numbers of places down the western slope, but near the ravines, the surface is dotted with the little gravestones. In some places, far down the descent, and far from where Custer, Van Reilly, Tom Custer, and others fell, they are seen singly; in other spots, three, or four, or half-a-dozen. At one point there are over thirty, well massed together. Down in this part of the field, in the ravine running toward the monument, is the stone marking where Dr. Lord's body was found, and with it are four others.

In the shallow coulée east of the ridge, and almost at the bottom of the slope, some distance northwest of where Calhoun and Crittenden were killed, and on the main ridge slope of it, is a large group of stones. Here is where Capt. Myles Keogh and thirty-eight men gave up their lives. On this side of the ridge — the eastern side — between where Keogh and his men died and where Custer fell, there are numerous stones. On the opposite side of the Custer ridge — that which faces the river — and close to its crest, there are very few stones, and those are much scattered, and not in groups.

At the northern extremity of the ridge is a slight elevation which overtops everything else, and slopes away in all directions, save where the ridge lies.

Just below this 'knoll, or hillock — Custer Hill — facing southwest, is where Custer and the larger part of his men fell.

Looking toward the river, to Custer's right, Capt. Yates died; at the left, Lieut. Van Reilly. Below Van Reilly, Lieut. Smith dropped, and above Custer and a little to the right, Capt. Tom Custer fell. Farther down the slope, to the right, Boston Custer and Autie Reed were killed. Some of the stones face toward the north, others to the east.

Since the battle-ground was converted into a national cemetery many interments from other places have been made. There are now interred here 657 besides those of the Custer fight.

THE OUTWARD MARCH.

On the right bank of the Missouri River — the Big Muddy — in North Dakota, almost within rifle-shot of the town of Mandan, on the Northern Pacific Railroad, there existed in the '70's a military post named after the nation's great martyr president, Fort Abraham Lincoln.

On the morning of the 17th of May, 1876, there went forth from here among others, with the pomp and ceremony of war for which they were distinguished, a cavalry regiment famed in the annals of the army for dash, bravery, and endurance — the noted Seventh Cavalry.

In command of this force, and also of another operating in conjunction with it, was Gen. Alfred H. Terry, the lawyer-soldier and gentleman.

At the head of the Seventh Cavalry was a man who was unquestionably the most picturesque character for long years, and perhaps for all previous and present time, in the army. Entering the army in active service during the Civil War, his career was a continual round of successes and advances, and at its close, aside from the peerless Sheridan, no cavalryman had a greater reputation for magnificent dash than he.

Transferred to the plains — the war over — his success as an Indian campaigner naturally followed, and at the time he moved out upon his last and fated expedition, George A. Custer had a reputation as an Indian fighter second to none.

He started upon this scout under a cloud. While in Washington, a slight, whether fancied or real, toward Gen. Grant — then president — had resulted in his military arrest, and only upon the intercession of Gen. Terry, warmly seconded by Sheridan, who was a stanch friend of his, had he been released and permitted to join his regiment on the very eve of departure.

The story of Custer's last march is graphically told, and in much detail, by Capt. — then Lieutenant — E. S. Godfrey, in the *Century* for January, 1892. Powder River was reached on the evening of June 7th. At this point Gen. Terry went up the Yellowstone River to consult Gen. Gibbon who was coming from Fort Ellis, Mont., with a co-operating force.

Returning to the column Gen. Terry gave orders for a scout up the Powder River Valley. This work was intrusted to Maj. M. A. Reno.

From the mouth of Powder River, Custer, with six companies, scouted over into the Tongue River Valley. On the 19th word was received from Reno that he had discovered a very heavy Indian trail, which he had followed for forty miles.

Custer and Reno's commands were now consolidated again, and on June 21st reached the mouth of the Rosebud River.

At this point, at a conference on board the steamer Far West between Terry, Gibbon, and Custer, the former unfolded his plan of campaign.

It appears to have been, in a general way, that of converging columns, a plan strongly condemned in all usual military operations, generally disastrous in its results, and almost only justified by its success — an unusual thing. It would seem to have been, for several reasons, the proper thing to do here; had been eminently successful in previous Indian campaigns; and *might* have been successful now had Custer adhered more specifically, as many think, to the spirit of his instructions as they are known to us.

According to Capt. Godfrey's account there seem to have been a good many presentiments that things were going to turn out in an ill-fated way. Some believed that Custer himself felt that this was his last scout and service — that he was riding with Death's presence hovering near. Might it not have been true?

I have stated that many believe that had Custer not departed from the spirit of his instructions the disaster to him might not have occurred. Custer *disobeyed no orders*, and did only what nine out of ten men having his experience and possessed of his temperament and characteristics, and with the knowledge of the situation then at hand, would have been strongly tempted to do.

Terry hampered him with no *absolute* orders. He knew full well the danger of such a procedure on an expedition like Custer's, where conditions and surroundings could not possibly be foreseen, and where latitude, at least within reasonable limits, was absolutely essential. He did, however, give him written instructions, in which he indicated what his own views were, and *wished them to be conformed to*, unless Custer saw *good reason* for departing from them. Custer exercised the latitude thus allowed, whether wisely or not is the question.

Capt. Charles King, that prolific and most readable writer of army fiction, contributed to the August number of *Harper's Magazine*, in 1890, a decidedly interesting paper, entitled "Custer's Last Battle." Here is an excerpt from it:

"His orders" [Terry's] "to Custer displayed an unusual mingling of anxiety and forbearance. He seems to have feared that Custer would be rash, yet shrank from issuing a word that might reflect upon the discretion or wound the high spirit of his gallant leader of horse."

On June 22d Custer and the Seventh Cavalry left camp on the Rosebud in compliance with these instructions. On the 23d and 24th many of the camping places of the Indians, in their migration westward, were passed.

By evening of June 24th the trail and signs had become so hot and fresh that a halt was ordered to await tidings from the scouts. Their information proved that the Indians were across the divide, over in the valley of the Little Horn.

Custer, confident of his ability to whip the Indians single-handed, prepared for fight at once.

To quote again from King, " He pushed ahead on the trail, .   .   .   and created the impression that it was his determination to get to the spot and have one battle royal with the Indians, in which he and the Seventh should be the sole participants on our side, and by consequence the sole heroes.   The idea of defeat seems never to have occurred to him.   .   .   ."

Custer and his men were again in the saddle at 11 or 11:30 P. M., and marched until 2 A. M. of the 25th.

Custer's original plan was to have surprised the Indian city in the early morning of the 26th. They had now, however, been seen by the Indians, and believing that surprise was impossible, preparations for a daylight attack on the 25th were made.

Had it been possible for the first conceived plan to have been carried into effect, the result would probably have been very different. The method of attack was the same in both cases, save the essential difference in the *time* at which it was to have been made and was actually made. It was one that had been previously used by not only Custer himself, but also others, and with very great success.

THE BATTLE.

Early on the morning of June 25th Custer resumed his march. Up to that time the command was maneuvered as a whole. Now, however, it was divided into four detachments. One under Maj. Reno, consisting of three troops of cavalry and the Indian scouts, forty in number, held the advance; a second battalion under Capt. Benteen, composed also of three troops, moved off some miles to the left of Reno, scouting the country to the southward; a third detachment, comprising the pack train which carried the reserve ammunition — some 24,000 rounds — was under the command of Capt. McDougall, and had one troop as an escort; the fourth battalion was that under Custer himself, and was the largest, having five troops, and it marched parallel to Reno and within easy supporting distance to the north, the pack train following the trail in rear of Reno and Custer.

The troops are said to have averaged about forty-five men each, which would give the relative numbers approximately as follows:

```
Custer _____225
Reno _____135
Benteen _____135
McDougall _____ 45
                                                            ___
       Total_____540
```

The divide between the Rosebud and the Little Big Horn seems to have been crossed about noon, and the division of the command made shortly afterward.

Some miles from the Reno ford a burning tepee, containing the dead body of an Indian — stated to have been that of Turning Bear, a brother-in-law of Sitting Bull — was passed.

Not far from the river, Reno received orders "to move forward at as rapid a gait as prudent, and to charge afterward, and that the whole outfit would support him." No mention was made as to just when, where, or how that support would be given; whether by following in his wake or by attacking the village at another point.

Reno móved off to the river at a trot, crossed it, and used about ten minutes in watering horses and getting the battalion in order to advance, after the disarrangement consequent on fording the river and watering the horses.

Reno advanced from the ford across the valley in column of fours for some distance, then formed in line of battle, and afterward deployed the command as skirmishers.

The bulk of the Indians and their camp were hidden by a bend of the river, and Reno, instead of charging around the bend and into the Indian camp, halted and dismounted his command to fight on foot. At this point two or three of the horses could not be controlled, and carried their riders into the Indian camp; one account stating that they plunged over the river bank, some thirty feet high, into the river, injuring the men who were afterward killed by the Indians.

Here at Ash Point, or Hollow, the command soon got sheltered in the timber, and were on the defensive, the Indians now pouring in from all sides. The Ree Indian scouts with Reno had before now been dispersed, and were making back tracks as fast as their ponies could carry them. Accounts differ as to how long they remained in this timber, but it was probably not to exceed half an hour. The "charge" out — as Reno termed it — was virtually a stampede, and many did not know of the departure until too late to start, no well-defined and well-understood order having been given to that effect.

There was no systematic attempt to check the pursuit of the Indians who now, directed by Gall, swarmed down upon them and prevented them from reaching the ford at which they had crossed. Many were killed on this retreat, and many others wounded, among the former being Lieut. Donald McIntosh. Reno headed the retreat, and they tore pell mell across the valley, and at the new ford they were lucky to strike there was great confusion, it being every man for himself and the devil take the hindmost; and, as is usually the case, the (red) devil got his clutches on more than one. Crossing the stream as best they could, Lieut. Hodgson being killed after having crossed, men and horses climbed the steep, almost inaccessible, clay bluffs and ravines, upon the top of which they had a chance to "take account of stock." Many had attempted to scale the bluffs at other points hard by. The Indians were up there in some force, and by them, when almost up the cliffs, Dr. De Wolf was killed.

Some have thought that Reno should have remained sheltered in the timber, but there can be little if any doubt that the wise course was, under all the circumstances, to get to the bluffs as he did. Whether he made this move with any definite purpose or thought in mind, other than simply a desire to get away from there, is doubtful.

And now, what of Custer?

How fared it all this time with Long Hair and his brave troopers? There is really little to be told that is absolutely known, but much to be conjectured.

Martin, or Martini — whichever it may be — Custer's trumpeter, is the only man of his battalion that accompanied him on his ride after the division of the command, and returned to the other troops.

His story in brief is, that soon after Reno trotted away from them at the burning tepee, Custer turned to the right or north, and followed up the hills to the top of the ridge.

From a point on the ridge they overlooked a portion of the valley below, and some part, but not by any means the larger part, of the Indian encampment. According to the trumpeter the village appeared to be asleep, and Custer, elated at the prospect, pulled off his hat, waved it about his head and shouted: "Courage, boys! We have got them. As soon as we get through we will go back to our station."

They then left the bluff ridge, and shortly afterward Custer instructed Adj. Cook to write the now well-known order to Benteen:

"Benteen, come on. Big village. Be quick. Bring packs."

"P. S. Bring packs."

Cook stopped and wrote the message, and the trumpeter turned back on the trail, leaving Custer going down the coulée at a gallop. Hastening ahead, he met Benteen in the valley of Sundance, or Reno, Creek, delivered the message, and with him joined Reno on the hills.

This story of the trumpeter is partially corroborated by the fact that some of Reno's men saw three men and a marching column on the bluffs just before Reno left the timber.

Beyond this no man lived after Custer's battle who could tell what was done after the trumpeter left him. All else was and·is pure speculation, based upon the supposed trail followed by Custer and the stories of the Indians who fought him. The latter have cleared up many things previously unknown, and changed radically the theories at first held regarding the nature of the action.

Let us now return to Reno.

After remaining on the bluffs at least an hour, probably longer, a forward movement down stream was made for a mile or mile-and-a-half. Previous to this, heavy firing had been heard down the river in the direction Custer had gone. Two distinct volleys were heard by the entire command, followed by scattering shots, and it was supposed Custer was carrying all before him.

When Reno had reached the limit of this advance north toward Custer, they saw large numbers of Indian horsemen scurrying over what afterward proved to be Custer's battle-field. Soon these came tearing up toward Reno, who hastily retreated from what would seem to have been a strong position back to near the point where he had originally reached the bluffs. Here they sheltered themselves on the small hills and nubs by shallow breastworks, and placed the wounded and horses in a depression. That night until between 9 and 10 o'clock they were subjected to a heavy fire from the Indians, who entirely surrounded them. The firing again began at daylight of the 26th, and lasted all day, and as the Indians had command of some high points near by there were many casualties. Reno's total loss, as given by Godfrey, was fifty killed, including three officers, and fifty-nine wounded. Many of those left in the river bottom when the retreat began eventually reached the command again, escaping under cover of night.

On the evening of the 26th the Indians, knowing of Terry's advance up the Little Horn valley, hastily decamped to the west with their immense pony herds, tepees, etc.

On the morning of the 27th Terry and Gibbon arrived, and then for the first time Reno and his men learned that Custer and his five troops had been cut to pieces.

Of Custer's movements after the trumpeter left him, opinions as to what he did or should have done are many and various.

The theory first entertained and held for years, but not now tenable nor, indeed, probably held by many, was that Custer reached the ford and attempted to cross; was met by a fire so scorching that he drew back and retreated to the hill in the best form possible; and there fought like an animal at bay, hoping that Reno's attack in the bottom and Benteen's timely arrival would yet relieve him.

The Indians, however, strenuously assert that Custer *never attempted the ford, and never got anywhere near it.*

No dead soldiers' bodies were found nearer than within half-a-mile of the ford, and it seems undoubted that the Indians tell the truth.

What then did Custer do, and if he never got near the ford, why was it ?

Capt. Godfrey gives Custer's trail — based upon his own observations and Chief Gall's statements — as running far back from the first line of bluffs on the river, diagonally over to the second line, to a point *two miles* from the ford, thence at right angles to Custer Hill.

This seems preposterous, for it is not by any means the natural route to the ford, nor to Custer Hill, and if it was the trail there was a weighty reason for it.

What was it ?

When Custer rode out on the bluffs and looked over into the valley of the Greasy Grass, he must have seen at once that he had before utterly misapprehended the situation. The natural thing to do would have been to retrace his trail, join Reno by the shortest route, and then, united, have pushed the attack in person, or if then too late for successful attack he could, in all likelihood, have extricated the command, and made junction with Terry.

But having started in as he had he did not want to draw back.

Indian signals travel rapidly, and as soon as Reno was checked and beaten, not only was this fact signaled through the camp, but every warrior tore away down stream to oppose Custer, joining those already there, and now at least alert.

Is it improbable then, that before Custer could reach the creek valley the Indians had made sufficient demonstrations to have caused him to swerve from where he would otherwise, and naturally, strike it, and work farther back toward the second line of bluffs, even perhaps as far back as Capt. Godfrey gives the trail ? The only thing to militate against this would be the element of time, which seems hardly to oppose it.

However he got there, Custer is at last upon the eminence which is to be so soon consecrated with his life's blood.   .

What saw he, what did he ?   The sources of information are necessarily largely Indian. At the southeastern end of the Custer ridge facing, apparently, the draw, or coulée, of the branch of Custer Creek, Calhoun and Crittenden were placed. Some little distance back of them, in a depression, and down the northern slope of the Custer ridge, Keogh stood. Stretched along the north slope of the ridge from Keogh to Custer Hill was Smith's command, and at the culminating point of the ridge, or Custer Hill, *but on the opposite side of the ridge* from where the others were placed, were Tom Custer and Yates and, with them, Custer himself. Yates' and Custer's men faced evidently north-northwest. It would appear from the Indians' statements that most of the command were dismounted.

The line was about three-quarters of a mile in length.

The attack was made by two bodies of Indians. One, coming up from the so-called Custer ford, wound around through the shallow coulée, leading up from it to the northward of the command, and, led by Gall with his Uncapapas, charged over and crushed out Calhoun and Keogh, and then, like a resistless tornado, bore down upon Smith and the others. Calhoun and his men fell in several spots, as if deployed as skirmishers. Keogh and most of his men fell in one big bunch.

The other body of Indians came up from the valley lower down the river, and, led by Crazy Horse with his fighting Cheyennes, swarmed up the coulées to the northwest and bore down upon Custer and Yates and Smith, and then the two columns intermingled and, circling around, completed the destruc-

BAD LANDS.

CUSTER BATTLE FIELD.

tion of the command. Between the ridge and the river the Indians came not. Down over this space toward the rough ravines, in various directions, fled many of the men, hoping to find hiding spots until the night should give them opportunity to escape. But after them streamed Cheyenne, Uncapapa, Ogalalla, Brulé, and the rest, and every man was sooner or later cut down; not one living thing, save Capt. Myles Keogh's horse Comanche, escaping from the slaughter. I say not *one* living thing besides him escaped.

For a long time it was told and believed that the Crow scout Curley, watching his chance, disguised himself in a Sioux blanket and finally got away. This story is apocryphal. Without citing the evidence, it is now disbelieved by many, and I am convinced that Curley "snuffed the battle from afar," and was, as a matter of fact, not in the fight.

From the Indian accounts it is probable that the fight was practically over within half an hour.

My guide stated that Wah-to-pah — an Assinaboine, an adopted son of Sitting Bull, born of white parents, and captured when a child — told him that he knew Custer, and that as they were circling about him he saw Custer lying on the ground wounded. That the third time that they went around, Pah-hoska — Long Hair — had a blanket spread entirely over him, and that he thought he was then dead.

Sitting Bull, who it can now scarcely be doubted was *not in the fight at all*, but was fleeing for dear life, informed my guide, so he said, that there were 163 Indians dead in front of Custer, and a great many were wounded.

The entire losses of Custer's and Reno's commands were 265 killed and 52 wounded. There were buried considerably more than 200, while there were a number of bodies, both of officers and men, never recognized.

Since the first part of this narrative was written I have received from Maj. James McLaughlin — Indian agent at Standing Rock Agency, Fort Yates, N. D. — a letter in answer to certain inquiries I made. This letter contains so much, and states it so well, that I incorporate it here almost entire, as a valuable, and in many things probably a new, addition to the literature and knowledge on this subject:

UNITED STATES INDIAN SERVICE.
STANDING ROCK AGENCY,
FORT YATES, N. D., Oct. 20, 1892.

It is difficult to arrive at, even approximately, the number of Indians who were encamped in the valley of the Little Big Horn when Custer's command reached there on June 25, 1876; the indifference of the Indians as to ascertaining their strength by actual count, and their ideas at that time being too crude, to know themselves. I have been stationed at this agency since the surrendered hostiles were brought here in the summer of 1881, and have conversed frequently with many of the Indians who were engaged in that fight, and more particularly with Gall, Crow King, Big Road, Hump, Crow, Sitting

Bull, Gray Eagle, Spotted Horn Bull, and other prominent men of the Sioux regarding the Custer affair, and when questioned as to the number of Indians engaged, the answer has invariably been: " None of us knew, *nina wicoti*," which means very many lodges. From this source of information, which is the best obtainable, I place the number of male adults then in that camp at 3,000; and that on June 25, 1876, the fighting strength of the Indians was between 2,500 and 3,000, and more probably approximating the latter number.

Sitting Bull was a recognized medicine man, and of great repute among the Sioux; not so much for his powers of healing and curing the sick — which after he had gained such renown was beneath his dignity — as for his prophecies; and no matter how absurd his prophecies might be, he found ready believers and willing followers, and when his prophecies failed to come to pass he always succeeded in satisfying his over-credulous followers by giving some absurd reason. For instance, I was in his camp on Grand River in the spring of 1888, sometime about the end of June. There had been no rain for some weeks, and crops were suffering from drought, and I remarked to him, who was in an assemblage of a large number of Indians of that district, that the crops needed rain badly, and that if much longer without rain the crops would amount to nothing. He—Sitting Bull—replied: " Yes, the crops need rain, and my people have been importuning me to have it rain. I am considering the matter as to whether I will or not; I can make it rain any time I wish, but I fear *hail*. I can not control hail, and should I make it rain, heavy hail might follow, which would ruin the prairie-grass as well as the crops, and our horses and cattle would thus be deprived of subsistence." He made this statement with as much apparent candor as it was possible for a man to give expression to, and there was not an Indian among his hearers but appeared to accept it as within his power.

Sitting Bull was dull in intellect, and not near as able a man as Gall, Hump, Crow, and many others who were regarded as subordinate to him; but he was an adept schemer and very cunning, and could work upon the credulity of the Indians to a wonderful degree, and this, together with great obstinacy and tenacity, gained for him his world-wide reputation.

Sitting Bull claimed in his statement to me that he directed and led in the Custer fight; but all the other Indians with whom I have talked contradict it, and say that Sitting Bull fled with his family as soon as the village was attacked by Maj. Reno's command, and that he was making his way to a place of safety, and several miles out in the hills, when overtaken by some of his friends with news of victory over the soldiers, whereupon he returned, and, in his usual style, took all the credit of victory to himself as having planned for the outcome, and as having been on a bluff overlooking the battle-field, appeasing the evil spirits and invoking the Great Spirit for the result of the fight. And when considering the ignorance and inherent superstition of the average Sioux Indian at that time, it is not to be wondered at that the majority, if not all, were willing to accept it, especially when united in common cause and what they considered as their only safety from annihilation. As a matter of fact, there was no one man who led or directed that fight; it was a "pell mell" rush under a number of recognized warriors as leaders, with Gall of the Hunk-papas and Crazy Horse of the Cheyennes the more prominent.

Sitting Bull had a pair of twin-boys born about that time; one of them died about a year ago, and the other is yet living. He—Sitting Bull—denied having left one of these boys behind in his camp, but admitted that his family had gotten separated; and that the story of his being in the hills during the fight was accounted for by his absence, for a time, in searching for the missing members of his family.

The Indians with whom I have talked deny having mutilated any of the killed, but admit that many dead bodies were mutilated by women of the camp; and they also claim that the fight with Custer was of short duration. They have no knowledge as to minutes and hours, but have explained by the distance that could be walked while the fight lasted, and they vary from twenty minutes to three-quarters of an hour, none placing it longer than forty-five minutes. This does not include the fight with Reno before his retreat, but from the time the second command—Custer's—advanced, and the fight with his command commenced.

The opinion of the Indians regarding Reno's first attack and short stand at that point all agree that it was his retreat that gave them the victory over Custer's command. The "helter-skelter" retreat of Reno's command enthused the Indians to such an extent that, flushed with excitement and this early success, they were reckless in their charge upon Custer's command, and with the large number of Indians thus fully enthused that small command was but a slight check to their sweeping impetuosity. The Indians also state that the separated detachments made their victory over the troops more certain.

From these statements it would appear:

1st. That had Custer gone into the fight with his entire command united, he would, in all probability, have fought out a victory.

2d. That had Reno pushed his attack from the first, vigorously and with dash, the same result *might* have come.

3d. That the number of Indians was far in excess, from three to five times greater, than the military had any knowledge of, and, it may be added, increasing every day.

It is generally agreed that Custer's body was not in the least mutilated. He was shot in the side and temple.

Regarding the wisdom of Custer's attack at all, there are, and probably always will be, conflicting opinions. There seem to be good arguments for both sides.

Regarding Custer's valor, ability, and the honor due his memory, there can be but one opinion. His candle of life was too soon snuffed out, under circumstances that surround his and his brave men's death with a halo of glory, an appropriate ending to a soldier's career.

The foregoing pages are the result of an extended journey through the country tributary to the Northern Pacific Railroad, in the summer of 1892.

The writer is under obligations in one way and another, to many persons for courtesies extended personally and officially, information given, papers and documents loaned, etc. He desires herewith to thank one and all for favors rendered, and trusts that those among them who may chance to peruse what he has written, may feel that their kindness was not wholly thrown away.

O. D. W.

NORTHERN PACIFIC R. R.

Rates and Arrangements for the Tourist Season.

MINNESOTA SUMMER RESORTS.—The Northern Pacific Railroad will sell round-trip excursion tickets from St. Paul or Minneapolis to Glenwood (Lake Minnewaska) at $5 25; Battle Lake, $7.50; Fergus Falls, $7.50; Perham, $7.75; Detroit Lake, $9.15; Minnewaukan (Devil's Lake), $18.65; Winnipeg, $22.50. From Duluth or Superior to Battle Lake, $7.50; Fergus Falls, $7.50; Perham, $7.75; Detroit Lake, $9.15; Minnewaukan, $18.65; Winnipeg, $22.50. From Ashland, Wis., to Battle Lake, $9.00; Fergus Falls, $9 00; Perham, $9.25; Detroit Lake, $10.65; Minnewaukan, $20.15; Winnipeg, $22.50. Tickets on sale May 1st to September 30th, inclusive. Good going to Minnesota resorts one day (from Ashland two days), to Minnewaukan (Devil's Lake) and Winnipeg two days from date of sale. Good to return on or before October 31st.

YELLOWSTONE PARK RATES.—The Northern Pacific Railroad, the only rail line to the Park, will sell round-trip excursion tickets from May 29th to September 28th (both dates inclusive) at the following rates:

A $130.00 ticket, including the following traveling expenses, from St. Paul, Minneapolis, Duluth or Ashland on the east, and Portland, Tacoma, or Seattle on the west, to and through the Park (including Yellowstone Lake) and return to starting point, viz.: Railroad and stage transportation, Pullman sleeping car fares, meals on Northern Pacific dining cars, and board and lodging at the Park Association Hotels six and one-quarter days.

A $50 00 round-trip ticket, St. Paul, Minneapolis, Duluth, or Ashland to Livingston and return.

A $12.50 ticket, Livingston to Mammoth Hot Springs Hotel and return, including rail and stage transportation, and one and one-quarter days' board at Mammoth Hot Springs.

A $60.00 ticket, Livingston to Cinnabar and return, Cinnabar to Mammoth Hot Springs, Norris, Lower and Upper Geyser Basins, Yellowstone Lake, Grand Cañon and Falls of the Yellowstone and return, including rail and stage transportation, and six and one-quarter days accommodations at the Association Hotels.

Limit and Conditions of Tickets.—The $130.00 Ticket will be on sale, at eastern and western termini named, May 29th to September 28th, inclusive; by eastern lines, May 28th to September 27th, limit 40 days; good going 30 days, returning 10 days, but must be used in the Park before October 6th. Stop-overs within final limit at or east of Billings, and at or west of Helena. Return portion of ticket must be signed and stamped at Mammoth Hot Springs Hotel, after which ticket must be presented on main line train for return passage within one day from such date. Stop-overs in Park granted at pleasure of holder within final limit of ticket.

Limit of $50.00 rail ticket, same as above. Stop-over privileges allowed within limits. Return portion of ticket must be stamped and signed at Livingston ticket office.

The $12.50 and $60.00 tickets, on sale at eastern and western termini between dates first named above, at Livingston May 31st to September 30th, both dates inclusive, are good if used in the Park any time between June 1st and October 6th, both dates inclusive, and do not require identification of purchaser.

The hotel service in the Park is now very complete. Tourists can stop at any of the principal points of interest with the assurance that comfortable accommodations will be supplied them.

MONTANA AND EASTERN WASHINGTON POINTS.—The Northern Pacific Railroad sells daily, round-trip excursion tickets to Bozeman at $55.00; Helena and Butte, $60.00 (choice of routes returning, via Northern Pacific, Union Pacific, or Great Northern Ry. Lines); Missoula, $62.50; Spokane, $70.00 (choice of routes returning, via Union Pacific, Great Northern, or Northern Pacific Lines); Medical Lake, $70.00; and Nelson, B. C., $70.00.

These tickets are of iron-clad signature form; require identification of purchaser at return starting point, limited to 90 days, good going 40 days and returning 40 days. Stop-overs granted at any point within limits stated.

To Springdale (Hunter's Hot Springs), Mont., and return, $50.00; on sale daily; good 40 days—going limit 30 days, return limit 10 days.

NORTH PACIFIC COAST EXCURSIONS.—An $80.00 round-trip individual excursion ticket, St. Paul, Minneapolis Duluth or Ashland to Tacoma, Portland, Seattle or Victoria, is on sale daily at points first named and by eastern lines.

Tacoma, Seattle, Victoria or Portland tickets, at above rates, will be issued, going via Cascade Division, returning via Columbia River Line, or vice versa; Portland tickets via either Cascade Division or Columbia River, returning via Union Pacific to either Omaha or Kansas City, or to St. Paul via Union Pacific Railway through Sioux City; and Victoria tickets good to return via Canadian Pacific to either Winnipeg, Pt. Arthur, St. Paul or Minneapolis.

CONDITIONS.—Above tickets limited to nine months from date of sale; good, going trip, 60 days to any one of North Pacific Coast termini named, returning any time within final limit.

ALASKA EXCURSIONS.—An excursion ticket will be sold from eastern termini named to Sitka, Alaska, at $175.00, which rate includes meals and berth on the steamer. Tickets on sale May 1st to September 30th. Limit nine months. Going to Tacoma, 60 days, returning within final limit, holder to leave Sitka on or before October 31st. Tickets will be issued to return either via the Northern Pacific or the Canadian Pacific and Great Northern Ry. Lines to St. Paul or Minneapolis. Usual stop-over privileges granted. Steamer accommodations can be secured in advance by application to any of the agents named below. Diagrams of steamers at office of General Passenger Agent at St. Paul.

"TO THE WESTWARD."—The Northern American Commercial Company's Mail steamer "Crescent City" will sail from Sitka for Dutch Harbor in Behring Sea, 1,500 miles distant, 9th of April, May, September, and October; 13th of June, July, and August. This makes close connection with the Pacific Coast Steamship Co.'s vessels "City of Topeka" and "Queen." This steamer has accommodations for 22 cabin passengers. Round trip is made in from 27 to 30 days, one week of which time is spent at Dutch Harbor, from which point a side trip is made to the Bogeslov Volcano, 40 miles distant. Round-trip rate from Sitka, including berth and meals on boat and board and lodging at the North American Fur Trading Co.'s new station at Dutch Harbor, $120.00.

A NOTABLE BOOK.—Perhaps the most interesting book yet written on Alaska is that from the pen of Mrs. General C. H. T. Collis, bearing the title "A Woman's Trip to Alaska," from the press of the Cassell Publishing Company, New York.

CALIFORNIA EXCURSION RATES.—The Northern Pacific Railroad will sell round-trip excursion tickets from St. Paul, Minneapolis, Duluth or Ashland, as follows:

To San Francisco, going via either the Cascade Division or the Columbia River to Portland, and the Shasta route or the ocean to San Francisco; returning same route, or by the southern lines to Council Bluffs, Omaha, Kansas City, Mineola or Houston, at $100.00; to New Orleans or St. Louis, at $106.00.

To Los Angeles, going via Portland and Shasta route, and returning same route into San Francisco in one direction, at $119.00; or going via Portland and Shasta route or steamer, and returning via Sacramento and Ogden to Council Bluffs, Omaha or Kansas City, at $109.50; to St. Louis, at $115.50.

To San Diego going via Portland, and rail through Los Angeles, and returning same route, into San Francisco in one direction, at $129.00; or going via Portland and Shasta route or steamer, and returning via Sacramento and Ogden to Council Bluffs, Omaha or Kansas City, or via southern lines to Kansas City, Mineola or Houston, at $109.50; to St. Louis, at $115.50.

Tickets returning from Los Angeles or San Diego, via Ogden, will be issued reading via San Francisco and Ogden, at rates $4.00 higher than returning via Sacramento and Ogden. Tickets via ocean include meals and berth on steamer.

At the eastern termini of the southern transcontinental lines, excursion tickets will be sold, or orders exchanged, for tickets to San Francisco, returning via either the Shasta route, the all-rail line to Portland, or the ocean and the Northern Pacific to St. Paul, Minneapolis, Duluth, or Ashland, at a rate $20.00 higher than the current excursion rate in effect between Missouri River points, Mineola or Houston and San Francisco. The steamship coupon includes first-class cabin passage and meals between San Francisco and Portland.

Return coupons reading from Missouri River points to Chicago or St. Louis will be honored from St. Paul or Minneapolis, either free, or with a small additional charge, according to route.

These excursion tickets allow nine months' time for the round trip; 60 days allowed for west-bound trip up to first Pacific Coast common point; return any time within final limit.

General and Special Agents.

A. D. CHARLTON, Assistant General Passenger Agent, 121 First St., Portland, Ore.
A. L. CRAIG, Assistant General Ticket Agent, St. Paul, Minn.
B. N. AUSTIN, Assistant General Passenger Agent, St. Paul, Minn.
E. R. WADSWORTH, General Agent, 210 South Clark St., Chicago, Ill.
GEO. R. FITCH, General Eastern Agent, 319 Broadway, New York City, N. Y.
C. B. KINNAN, Eastern Passenger Agent, 319 Broadway, New York City, N. Y.
A. D. EDGAR, General Agent, Corner Main and Grand Streets, Helena, Mont.
W. M. TUOHY, General Agent, 23 East Broadway, Butte, Mont.
R. A. EVA, General Agent, Duluth, Minn.
H. SWINFORD, General Agent, Railway Station, Water Street, Winnipeg, Manitoba.
A. ROEDELHEIMER, General Agent, corner High and Chestnut Sts., Columbus, O.
G. G. CHANDLER, General Agent, 621 Pacific Avenue, Tacoma, Wash.
I. A. NADEAU, General Agent, Seattle, Wash.
T. K. STATELER, General Agent, Pass. Dept., 638 Market St., San Francisco, Cal.

Traveling Passenger Agents.

C. E. BRAY, 15 State Street, Boston, Mass.
J. H. ROGERS, JR., 47 South Third Street, Philadelphia, Penn.
L. L. BILLINGSLEA, 47 South Third Street, Philadelphia, Penn.
GEO. D. TELLER, 44 Exchange Street, Buffalo, N. Y.
WM. G. MASON, 44 Exchange Street, Buffalo, N. Y.
D. W. JANOWITZ, 42 Jackson Place, Indianapolis, Ind.
A. A. JACK, 153 Jefferson Avenue, Detroit, Mich.
T. L. SHORTELL, 104 North Fourth Street, St. Louis, Mo.
J. J. FERRY, 132 Vine Street, Cincinnati, Ohio.
T. S. PATTY, Read Hotel, Chattanooga, Tenn.
JOHN N. ROBINSON, 100 Wisconsin Street, Milwaukee, Wis.
OSCAR VANDERBILT, 408 West Locust Street, Des Moines, Iowa.
THOS. HENRY, 126 St. James Street, Montreal, Canada.
THOS. RIDGEDALE, 83 York Street, Toronto, Ont.
T. D. CAMPBELL, 144 Superior Street, Cleveland, Ohio.
C. G. LEMMON, 210 Grand Central Station, Chicago, Ill.
FRANK O'NEILL, 121 First Street, Portland, Ore.
W. N. MEARS, 621 Pacific Avenue, Tacoma, Wash.
W. H. WHITAKER, St. Paul, Minn.
R. W. GLADING, Thomasville, Ga.

J. M. HANNAFORD,
General Traffic Manager.

CHAS. S. FEE,
General Passenger and Ticket Agent.

ST. PAUL, MINN.

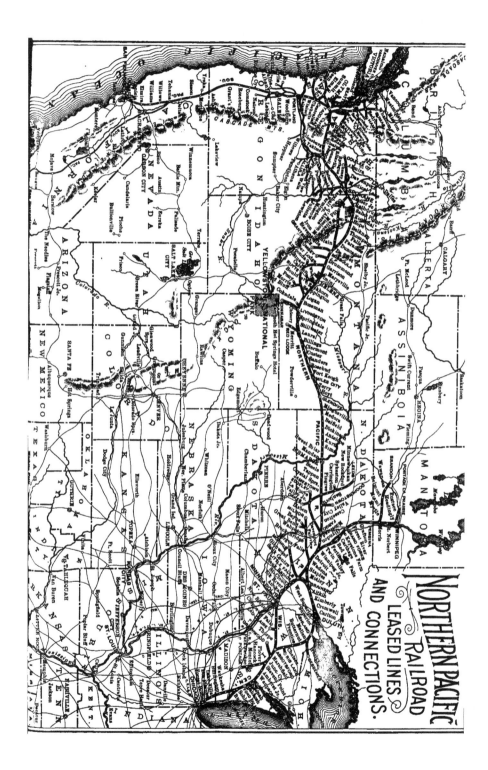

www.ingramcontent.com/pod-product-compliance
Lightning Source LLC
LaVergne TN
LVHW012202040326
832903LV00003B/63

* 9 7 8 1 3 5 8 2 8 0 6 3 4 *